Ex Ma

MW01005397

ESSAYS FROM THE EDGES OF SPECULATIVE FICTION

Edited by Chinelo Onwualu

HYDRA HOUSE BOOKS
THE CARL BRANDON SOCIETY

978-1-957898-00-1 (softcover)
978-1-957898-01-8 (hardcover)

Library of Congress Control Number: 2022952069

Hydra House Books
6204 Brewery Way
Lolo, MT 59847
http://www.hydrahousebooks.com/

All essays contained herein are original to the collection with the exception of the following:

"Unqualified," by Nisi Shawl, first appeared in *Cascadia Subduction Zone* (Vol. 5 No. 1—January 2015).

"Everything Else Is on Hold," by S.B. Divya, first appeared on the author's blog (December 1, 2021): https://sbdivya.com/fwords/2021/11/30/long-covid-disability-and-tough-decisions.

All works are copyrighted to their respective authors, and used here with their permission.

COVER ART by Ashe Samuels
BOOK DESIGN by Tod McCoy
PROOFREADING by Kate Dieda

First edition

Contents

Introduction
Writing Ourselves into Being

Chinelo Onwualu

I have often wondered what it must be like to be able to stretch the arms of my imagination and effortlessly find versions of myself at the tips of my fingers. To see myself continuously reflected in every media surface I turned to. If I knew—deeply and fundamentally—that my voice was valuable simply because I'd heard its song in every cadence and set to every beat, what sort of ease would that grant me? What sort of confidence? Would I still have the same bone-deep need for self-expression? And would that need be stymied by the same barriers—the crippling self-doubt, the paralyzing terror of getting it "wrong"?

I don't know. And honestly, I can't imagine it.

Because I have never had that privilege. Queer, dark-skinned black women like me are so routinely denied their basic humanity that when the rare piece of media bothers to represent us, we're often not even given the dignity of a full character arc.

I think that is why I was initially drawn to speculative fiction. Whenever reality became too much for me, I could escape into the wilds of outer space, into alternate dimensions and secondary worlds of magic, monsters, and myth where I hoped to find a version of me that I could wholly inhabit. It took me a long, long time to realize that that wasn't true. That even in the worlds of limitless imagination, imagining my humanity was just a stretch too far.

It has been a long, slow journey to personal value and recovery. A journey that has seen many, many fits and starts because it has required a kind of fundamental self-creation that I don't know that a lot of other people have to do—at least not in the same ways.

So, when I was asked to curate and edit a book of essays by speculative fiction authors from marginalized groups about the art, craft, and lived experiences of writing, I was excited but hesitant. I had no idea what I really wanted the collection to say. My initial, admittedly tepid, invitation to authors said that "we want to showcase whatever wisdom, passions, advice, and insights within the many intersections of your identity you want to share."

But I was wrong.

Over the two years it has taken me to put this anthology together, it has grown far beyond its initial scope. I wanted it to be a *Cri de Coeur* for speculative fiction writers whose identities have been historically and systematically disenfranchised. I wanted it to break down doors and scream in the faces of the genre's gatekeepers, insisting: "We are here! Hear us roar!" Instead, what I have is a nuanced, layered, and deeply personal collection that ranges from laugh-out-loud hilarious to thoughtful to heartbreaking.

I have been humbled by the breadth of talent that I have had the privilege to work with. Every author—whether they were able to make it into the final anthology or not—was a rare gem: breathtaking in beauty, priceless in value. Their stories reflect a vast spectrum of pain and joy and grace and growth. Yet, each one is a thoughtful depiction of what it means to produce creatively at every stage of a career, when the field wasn't built with you in mind.

Because one theme that emerged, over and over again, was that in order to see the full range of our diverse selves reflected in the speculative fiction we loved, too many of us had to write ourselves into existence—first on the margins of other people's stories, then in the tales we penned.

The idea for this anthology came at a time when parts of the Global North were reckoning with the legacies of anti-

Black racism that emerged out of their histories of human chattel slavery. Individuals and organizations were falling over themselves to affirm that Black Lives Matter and declare that they would be working towards meaningful change for Black people within their industries. The majority of those promises turned out to be nothing more than PR spectacles. This anthology, thankfully, has proven to be an exception to the trend.

Today, as many nations in the Global North inch dangerously closer to right-wing authoritarianism, their industries' commitments to reparative justice for all kinds of marginalized communities are evaporating. Many companies are scaling back their "diversity" initiatives or cancelling them altogether. Others are expanding to embrace regressive and reactionary voices. Will a similar trend overtake publishing? Who's to say. The industry has a long history of expansion and retraction when it comes to representing voices that aren't straight, white, or male.

There are so many people who I couldn't include in this collection—for a wide variety of reasons. I can only hope that they make it into the next one. Of course, I hope that there will *be* another one and that this won't be the only book of its kind.

Between a baby, a pandemic, and a breakup, this was a particularly difficult editorial process for me and the ever-patient team at Hydra House. But I have learned a lot about myself and my capacity, and I hope not to repeat my mistakes in the future.

So what happens next? Now that this book is a real thing out in the world—not just an abstract idea?

I ... don't know. I do hope that it starts some conversations, at least. That you, the readers, encounter a voice or an idea that resonates, and that you track down the author and their other writings. You won't regret it.

CHINELO ONWUALU
TORONTO, CANADA
DECEMBER 2022

Unqualified

Nisi Shawl

How good do you have to be to make it as a writer at this time, in this culture? A writer writing in standard English, a popular author whose work supports your existence? A writer who earns more than a pot to piss in and a window to throw it out of?

What if you want to stretch your talent further than that, even, and make a difference in the hearts and minds and souls of others—a difference in the world we all inhabit?

Do you think you're that good?

Most people of color don't. That's a problem.

There are so many obstacles to building a writing career, no matter what your race. I'm not going to claim poor self-esteem is our exclusive burden to bear, but I can tell you some of the ways it has affected me, and I can describe how this losing attitude is fostered among African Americans in particular, how we're constantly getting the message that we're unqualified for the work of creating a lasting literature—or even an interesting one.

And I can also discuss some ways to fix what's broken here.

Where to start? To paraphrase, the personal is historical—especially when you get to be my age. As a child in the 1960s, I was praised by the old folks for being "smart," which to them meant knowing lots of words. At the age of nine I could spell "antidisestablishmentarianism" and "supercalifragilisticexpialidocious." I could define infinity. My nickname was "Encyclopedia," just like the little white boy who solved mysteries in the books. But did anyone predict that I'd be able to write my own books? No. In their very wildest imaginings I would be accepted into a major college.

I was, to use the terminology of the period, a Negro. A "smart" Negro, who could get away with correcting her parents' pronunciation, who could absorb the lessons the predominantly white educational system taught. But absorption was as far as "smartness" would take me. No one dreamed I'd come up with my own lessons, deliver my own messages.

I recently read a review of a science fiction novel written in 1906 and featuring a "germicide for laziness" which was applied with good effect to "negroes." The unwillingness of my elders to dream big, to voice high ambitions for those in their community, resulted not from "laziness" but from persecution which reached its height not long after that novel appeared. Thriving Black farms and businesses were frequent targets of white supremacist terror. Doing well often meant dying horribly. The lynching of African Americans has continued on, occurring in the living memory of many, myself included. And the persecution I'm talking about extends beyond that outrage. When my mother was nine (the age at which I was dazzling older relatives with my etymological acumen), a black child, a boy of fourteen, was legally executed as a murderer in South Carolina.

"The squeaky wheel gets the grease," but "The nail that sticks up gets hammered down." Probably it was instilled wariness of standing out that kept my parents from putting me forward for arts programs designed to nurture creative children. In junior high school, I learned about Michigan's Interlochen Academy for the Arts and their Summer Arts Camps. They accepted students from third through twelfth grade. One of my white friends had attended; she was a violinist, but Interlochen also ran programs for writers. And I knew at a very early age I wanted to be a writer.

Instead, I got sent to Pretty Lake, a summer camp for "disadvantaged youth." During the pre-camp physical all of us had our heads searched for lice. I swam and wove potholders and advanced my literary career not one whit. Yet it wasn't until many years later, until after I dropped out of the major college my family was so proud to see me enter, that I wondered why I also had not been privileged to attend Interlochen.

It was a National Merit Scholarship that enabled me to attend the University of Michigan. That scholarship was based on my high SAT scores, but according to a close acquaintance (I can't really call him a friend), the reason I had been accepted as a student was so that black football players there would have someone to date.

This acquaintance's remark wasn't why I dropped out of college. I did so in large part because I didn't see any way for U of M to help me write—and especially to help me write science fiction and fantasy. Exposure to the feminist works of Joanna Russ, Suzy McKee Charnas, and Monique Wittig had taught me that this genre was where I could do what I wanted to do. And I wanted to do so much. I had dreams, ideas—but any talent I possessed with which to carry out those dreams went unrecognized by my teachers and the rest of the English and Creative Writing departments. I received no mentoring. There were grants I could have applied for, and fellowships, prizes, awards. I knew nothing about them, and heard nothing about them from anyone who did know. And I didn't ask for that kind of information, because I didn't believe literary grants and prizes were meant for me, despite my high SAT scores. It was all right to be ignorant of them, because they were obviously intended for "good" writers.

I almost didn't attend the Clarion West Writers Workshop for similar reasons. You can't get in if you don't apply, and I almost didn't apply. Fortunately, in 1991 I met two of the 1992 instructors: Pat Cadigan and John Shirley. Shirley read my work and encouraged me to go. At Clarion West I received six years' worth of education in six weeks. I made friends with other fledgling authors and some professional authors and editors. I earned respect for my abilities from people whose opinions mattered to me.

When the workshop ended I knew that I was a good writer. But I also still knew that I wasn't.

W.E.B. Dubois famously wrote about "double consciousness" as the disjunction between Black people's own experiences and their internalized understanding of how non-blacks view those same experiences. Something like this was at work in me, so that when Greg Bear didn't respond to my submission to the anthology he had announced to me and my Clarion West classmates, I assumed that my story had been rejected. In reality, it had been lost in the mail, as I realized after finally working up the nerve to ask him about it many years later. The story I sent around the same time to instructor Gardner Dozois, then editor at *Asimov's SF Magazine,* had been specifically requested by him, so it only took me a year to ask him whether he actually wanted it. He did, but I had to resend it. The first manuscript, as Dozois eventually discovered, had fallen behind a desk.

These sorts of missteps occur on every writer's path, I'm sure. But writers of color are more likely to lack the self-esteem necessary to correct them.

Low self-worth could well be a barrier to POCs attempting to write in any genre. With my longing to create imaginative worlds that refuse to default to the status quo, speculative fiction was obviously the field where I needed to focus my efforts. This field contained additional obstacles, though.

Science fiction, by my definition, is fiction that promotes science: its plot, settings, and characters are embedded in scientific values and scientific approaches to understanding the universe. The scientific method is easy to describe: you come up with a hypothesis to explain a phenomenon and you test it. You compare your results with those of others who perform identical tests. Simple, right? Anyone can do this.

And yet science itself is contested ground. Histories of science taught in the US spotlight the achievements of individual white males and downplay contributions by groups, women, and POC. Immigrants and the descendants of those brought to this country as slaves may see few images of scientists resembling themselves, just as they may see few images of writers—especially SF writers—who look similar. Worse, they may be taught that qualities the dominant culture assigns to their race are antithetical to science: passion, intuition, sensuality, spirituality, and so on. Assignment of these qualities is arbitrary, and of course, the idea that their presence prevents anyone from using the scientific method is nonsense, as any practicing scientist will tell you. But it is powerful nonsense, and it is often proffered as the truth. Finally, POC may be told that the proper subjects of scientific inquiry have nothing to do with their firsthand experiences and concerns. In some cases this stance relates to the hard/soft science dichotomy (social sciences such as anthropology are sometimes regarded as less legitimately scientific than—what should we call them, asocial sciences?—such as physics, chemistry, and the like).

All these factors serve to divorce POC from science and, by extension, from science fiction. As a girl geek in grade school, I studied molds and experimented with creating dyes, so later on I wasn't totally unfamiliar with the scientific paradigm. But to whatever extent I identified as a scientist, I felt I had to disavow my identities as a woman and POC. This circumscribed connection was what I had available. I worked with it. I worried, though. Was I a fraud, fronting, "passing" as scientifically literate? I worried even as I researched neuroplasticity in the human brain for a story about an imaginary drug, or as I pondered the geoavailability of rare earths in the mountains of Everfair, home of my Belgian Congo steampunk alternate history novel.

Much of what I've written sells as fantasy, not as science fiction. Fantasy has a wider market than science fiction: more readers enjoy it without knowing they're straying from the mainstream. Fantasy can be almost any fiction that doesn't mimic consensus reality. But it has its stock elements as well, its familiar tropes. Hardly any of these derive from the cultures of POC. European legends of King Arthur and his Roundtable anchor many a classic fantasy. Unicorns, elves, and wizards wearing pointy hats all spring from Europe's rich magical traditions. Dragons appear in Asian lore, but it's their European counterparts who soar and roar through the pages of most fantasies, from

Tolkien's *The Hobbit* through George R.R. Martin's A Song of Ice and Fire. Even the ostensibly mundane settings, characters, and props of the majority of fantasy fiction are undeniably European: the swords, the castles, the farms, the food. Medieval Europe was the default setting for fantasy for decades. Its stories and novels made very occasional (and at times problematic) excursions to more "exotic" locales (see *Kai Lung's Golden Hours* by English writer Ernest Bramah, published in 1922, for example).

Until very recently, POC fantasy writers basically had two choices. We could:

1. ignore the alienation implicit in creating worlds based on the traditions of our oppressors, or
2. write from our own heritage and have the results rejected by publishers or misclassified (usually as horror if ancestors—dead people—were involved).

A few POC authors such as Samuel R. Delany and Octavia E. Butler were able to buck the past's Euro-trope trend. Delany's Nevèrÿon series takes place in prehistory, in an unspecified land somewhere in the Fertile Crescent; Butler's *Kindred*, taught widely in colleges, is set firmly in the US's Antebellum South. Exceptions don't invalidate the norm, though, and the norm's whiteness has taken—and still takes—a heavy dose of self-esteem to challenge. Its presence hangs on via reading lists and curricula, whittling away at the sense of legitimacy POC writers strive to build within themselves. And though fantasy's palette, as it were, has broadened considerably in the last few years, writing a fantasy which deviates from tried-and-true formulas is by no means an assured path to having it published. Nor is having that kind of thing published an assured path to fame and success. We know this. We wonder if we're wrong for trying to write from our hearts, and we wonder if we're wrong for trying to write to the market. We doubt ourselves, whichever way we decide to go.

For more on the topic of the obstacles POC encounter when writing fantasy, please read deepad's excellent essay "I

Didn't Dream of Dragons," available online at http://deepad.
dreamwidth.org/29371.html.

As I write this essay, self-publishing is going for an end run
around the book industry's traditional gatekeepers. This has its
upsides and its downsides. I'm a word geek and a punctuation
nerd, and I have difficulty taking seriously some of the poorly
proofed and weakly edited texts self-publishing produces.
Their inconsistency demonstrates that these infelicities are
flaws, errors, not artistic choices. I can't stand them, and I wish
their authors had gotten the help they needed in making their
books fit to read, from proofers, editors—someone. Yet my own
experiences leave me certain that the field's predominantly white
editors dilute the presence of POC authors in the fantastic genres.

For instance, one of these rejected "Cruel Sistah" because
he couldn't credit the story's premise of murderous jealousy
triggered by a sibling's "good" straight hair. I had to submit it
elsewhere. I had to have the self-esteem to do that. Eventually
"Cruel Sistah" was included in a Year's Best reprint anthology,
but it might easily have never seen the light of day. Later, I
substantially altered a couple of passages in a second story,
"Wallamelon," because another editor felt that I hadn't made
clear the danger of the crime menacing my heroine in the black
neighborhood where it was set. This neighborhood, modeled on
the one where I grew up, was completely safe and middle class.
There was no crime. I had to make this explicit, to tell and not
merely show it.

Other suggestions, other changes, other rejections have
had their effect on my career and on the stories I will leave as my
legacy, and I'm sure the same is true for many more POC. Because
our narratives depart from those favored by the dominant culture,
they are subject to misreading, and this can be discouraging.

Here's the last area I want to touch on in my lament for self
esteem: "corrections" to the speech of POC characters.

There are some publications which state right in their
guidelines that they simply will not accept stories written in, or
including sections written in, dialect. Granted, dialect is difficult

to do well. It's easily prone to stereotyping and can devolve into meaningless Buckwheatisms à la Eddy Murphy's Saturday Night Live caricature. But the rhythms, pronunciations, idioms, and references of nondominant vernaculars can be beautiful, and anyone trying to represent nonwhite cultures will want to represent nonwhite speech patterns. Which means we'll never submit to publications barring such representation.

Those who don't start by warning authors away from writing in nonstandard English can still have problems with it. I've been told that an intelligent person would never speak in dialect. I've had deliberately dropped "gs" reinstated at the ends of my gerunds. I've had sentences which I constructed in a colloquially black word order rearranged so that they're more "grammatical." Even if the editor herself understands what you're doing, the proofreader may not. Sometimes it's possible to reverse these mistaken "corrections" at the galley stage. But going through page after page of them takes time, and a conviction that you knew what you were doing in the first place. Since so many POC lack that conviction, we may instead accept changes with which we disagree.

Now the fun part of this essay: how to fix what's wrong.

More models will help. It's easier to believe you can write speculative fiction when you can point to multiple POC who have done so: Nalo Hopkinson, Malinda Lo, David Anthony Durham, Thomas King, Tananarive Due, Steve Barnes, Ted Chiang, Hiromi Goto, and Vandana Singh, to name only a few.

Honesty on the part of working POC speculative fiction authors as to what our lives are like will give aspiring colleagues a realistic idea of what to expect of their careers. That will protect newcomers' self-worth. If you know that established authors are scrambling to pay their rent, if you hear book covers are being whitewashed en masse, if you read emails complaining that clueless interviewers ask racist questions, you're better prepared to respond when those sorts of things happen to you. Forewarned is forearmed. This book is a step in that direction. I also recommend joining the Carl Brandon Society (www.carlbrandon.org), and signing up for the CBS listserv, which hosts discussions about these topics, among others.

Giving POC more access to publication will help. My publisher is Aqueduct, a small press which has also printed two novels by African American speculative fiction author extraordinaire Andrea Hairston. Apex Books, Tachyon Publications, Night Shade, Small Beer, Arsenal Pulp—all are small presses making significant contributions to the expanding presence of POC in the fantastic genres. Perhaps their small size translates into greater flexibility, less conservative narrative choices, readier responsiveness to new and growing markets. I'd like to see us all supporting the efforts of small presses to offer speculative fiction by POC.

Although I've pointed out several ways in which our double consciousness contributes to our low self-worth and inhibits POC from writing science fiction and fantasy, I'll close with the observation that it also aids us in our work. The experience of being "Othered" is invaluable for anyone who wants to convey strangeness, cognitive dissonance, and immersion in a nonnative culture. Looked at in this light, the ability of POC to create a lasting literature of speculative fiction is not just pretty good. It is good: just plain, unqualified good.

Nisi Shawl is best known for fiction dealing with gender, race, and colonialism, including the 2016 Nebula finalist novel *Everfair*, an alternate history of the Congo. They're the coauthor of *Writing the Other: A Practical Approach* and a cofounder of the Carl Brandon Society, and they've served on Clarion West's board of directors for decades.

Shawl edited and co-edited *Strange Matings: Science Fiction, Feminism, African American Voices, and Octavia E. Butler* and *New Suns: Speculative Fiction by People of Color*. Their story collection *Filter House* co-won the 2008 James Tiptree, Jr./Otherwise Award. Additional awards include the World Fantasy Award, two Locus Awards, and FIYAH Magazine's Ignyte Award. A new story collection, *Our Fruiting Bodies*, appeared last fall from Aqueduct Press. A middle grade novel, *Speculation*, is forthcoming in February 2023 from Lee & Low. Shawl lives in Seattle, one block away from a beautiful, dangerous lake full of currents and millionaires.

In Visibility, We Find Hope

Ada Nnadi

I was surrounded by speculative imaginings before I knew what "speculative" fiction was. It was in the fantastic tales of the tortoise, hare, and other anthropomorphic characters of the animal kingdom. It was in the epics of a hero getting lost in a forest, conversing with spirits, then crossing seven rivers and seven forests for seven days and seven nights, to achieve a goal.

These elements of speculative fiction are more than just literary devices. They form facets of my cultural experience, coloring my beliefs and leaving traces on my worldview. They are present in Nollywood movies featuring the occult, in the cautionary tales of things I should and shouldn't do—especially at night. They were in the family stories of visits by ghosts, or of relatives whose sole purpose is to be a hindrance at every turn through metaphysical means.

I didn't have to look far for the fantastical. But the same could not be said for another part of me: my queerness.

My queerness started with curiosity. Growing up, same-sex attraction was treated as a deviance, a perversion. In school, it was gossip, a tag for boyish girls and effeminate boys. In church, people were praying against—or being delivered from—the spirit of homosexuality. And then there was me asking questions: What does it mean? How does it feel?

My curiosity scared me. I remember finding a DVD copy of *The L-Word* at a friend's place. After she told me it belonged to her aunt and—in that blasé manner only a pre-teen could pull off—that it was about "lesbians and their drama," I refused to look at it again. I didn't want to be tempted to take it home because I was afraid watching it would turn me gay.

In her TED Talk "The Danger of a Single Story," Nigerian feminist author Chimamanda Ngozi Adichie talks about how the information we're exposed to can make us prone to a single conception of a situation or a group. She cautions that these beliefs can be boxes that hem a people in, restraints that cut them off and prevent multitudes. This was my relationship with queerness.

The single story that defined homosexuality as a failure of character—that prevented it from being talked about outside the context of sex, promiscuity, and aberration—was ill-equipped to answer my questions or help me get a handle on what I was feeling. So I kept my questions to myself, carrying with me the only reality in which queerness was permissible: a distant abnormality.

Imagine my confusion and surprise when—at twelve—in a book that documented responses from American teenagers about their embarrassing moments and first crushes, I read an entry about a girl liking another girl. It hadn't occurred to me that girls could simply have crushes on other girls—that homosexuality could also be as ordinary as embarrassing yourself in front of someone you liked.

It would be years later, at seventeen, in the first year of a law degree I would eventually abandon, that I found another positive representation of homosexuality. In *Orphan Black*, a science-fiction drama about clones, the love story between one clone and her female love interest is depicted with gentleness. The buildup and tenderness of their first kiss broke open a yearning in me.

Seventeen was also the age I had my first "real" crush on a girl. In the books I'd read, crushes were loud, passionate, and angsty things. That was how I recognized my first crush on a boy when I was eleven, and the reason I couldn't deny this one. But before all of that, there were the numerous instances of fierce protectiveness and warm tenderness toward girls at different points in my life. These feelings would consume me before I realized what was happening, yet I chalked them up to my desire to be really, *really* good friends with them. However, I didn't just want to be really good friends with this girl. Filled with the newfound yearning born from the love story, I wanted us to kiss too.

⁕

I began writing simply because I could. I was perhaps nine when I wrote my first story: A retelling of *Cinderella* set in a precolonial Nigerian village. I was surrounded and enthralled by stories, so it was only natural that I'd want to tell my own.

Finding Wattpad, an online literary platform for original stories, when I was in secondary school felt like stepping into a different world. I was overcome with frenzy when I discovered I could upload my own stories on the site. I was no longer restricted to diligently writing my stories in notebooks then making my mother, friends, neighbors, and classmates read them. Strangers on the internet, who *wanted* to, could read them too. My evenings and weekends were spent at a cybercafe trying to update my work on Wattpad because my Nokia Asha was not up for the task.

However, even though I lived in Nigeria, many of my stories focused on white people in American high schools. I did feature Nigerian characters, but it was the straight, white teenagers who were falling in love, having sex, and suffering from mental illnesses. They were the ones making deals with Lucifer and treating the Creator like their best friend. They were buying haunted houses and befriending ghosts.

There were certainly people who looked like me in the media I was exposed to; I had been brought up on work made for and by people who looked like me—and yet ...

In Nigeria, at the time, stories always seemed to follow the same format, the same themes. There was a dearth of nuance to the telling, despite the multiplicity of experiences being depicted. It was rare to find stories—especially contemporary ones—whose speculative elements weren't demonized; if there was juju, it was being used for bad things. There was a limit on the things a Nigerian character—a Nigerian teenager—could be. They only existed within the framework of moral messages. The evils they triumphed over were usually of the didactic, religious kind, or of economic hardship, and always due to their virtuousness. They weren't given the space to do weird, epic, wonderful things. If their behavior or appearance deviated from the norm, that feature was squashed by the end of the story and attributed to an evil supernatural power.

The situation appeared different for American characters—American teenagers. They could do *anything*, without judgment or consequences. Their stories were varied and multifaceted, and so I made them the medium for all the things I was unable to imagine my Nigerian characters doing—all the things that they could not be. Which is why the first queer character I wrote was white.

American books showing queer, usually white, teenagers having crushes, falling in love, and freely living their lives made it all seem normal. Their everyday depictions helped me piece it all together and make sense of my own queerness. But I wanted more: a community, accounts from queer people who looked like me. I wanted to see stories of queer Nigerians reflected in Nigerian media.

Straddling multiple identities—Black, African, queer, female—I've had to make compromises in order to see myself fully represented in media because it was almost impossible to find the range of my identities in any one place. My country and its media refused to see people like me, and on the rare times that it chose to, it was with disgust, criminalization, and death.

If I have to pick and choose which aspect of myself to put aside just so I can occupy space, to exist, then the conclusion must be that I do not matter. And if I do not matter, how can I look forward to better things?

I found authors Chimamanda Ngozi Adichie, Nnedi Okorafor, and Chinelo Okparanta at different points in my life, but they were each huge influences in my journey towards learning to write my whole self.

Adichie showed me that I could write stories that were enjoyable without being moralistic. Her debut novel, *Purple Hibiscus*, was assigned reading when I was in secondary school. In the main character and her family, I saw realities I recognized—that reflected me and the people I knew. Despite being set in the 1980s, it felt like a contemporary story about Nigerian teenagers being teenagers.

Through Okorafor, I found a world where whiteness did not have to be the vehicle through which I could explore contemporary speculative fiction. Her trio of Binti novellas opened a door for me: I didn't have to let the rules I had been brought up with hold me back. My Black African characters could do all that they wanted on their own.

Under the Udala Trees, Okparanta's coming-of-age novel about a queer girl coming to terms with her sexuality, offered me a mirror. It was my experiences reflected back at me, showing me that there was something to look forward to. That I was something to look forward to. It gave me the nudge to write that possibility into being.

With these three authors as a starting point, I searched for other writers who were also doing this work. The more writers I found, the more I felt seen, and the less compromises I had to make. When I wrote "Tiny Bravery" in 2020, I knew I wanted to write a tender queer story about two girls becoming friends and something more along the way. I had seen the *X-Men* cartoons and movies and had always thought about putting a Nigerian spin on mutants and superpowers. It wasn't either/or. I knew what I wanted and it was Nigerian and queer.

The existence of queer people on the African continent has been denied because all traces of us were erased, altered, or made inaccessible to the average person. The names for what we are were wiped out of our histories. Writing my identities into my work, to announce my presence and take up space, speaks back to that lost history. I am adding to that canon, recording new ones, and (re)discovering myself and others like me in my culture, mythology, and folklore.

Standing on the shoulders of all the creatives who have inspired me made me what I am today. Now whoever reads me—especially those whose experiences I'm speaking to—doesn't have to make the compromises it took me to get here.

We matter. We belong. We cannot only look forward to better things, we can take them for ourselves. It is what we deserve.

Ada Nnadi is a tired psychology student praying the Nigerian government lets them get their degree so they're one step closer to gaining the ability to read minds. They're doing a very awful job of being hard at work on their novel, but some of their short fiction has appeared in *Omenana, Anathema, Giganotosaurus*, and Tordotcom's 2022 anthology, *Africa Risen*. They will one day be the mother of many cats, two birds (because that's the closest they'll ever have to getting a pet dinosaur), one snake—and maybe a small dog.

Oja Oyingbo
Centering the Fringes

Ayòdélé Olófintúádé

I grew up in a family full of stories. From children just learning how to string their sentences together to the ancients who could barely remember their own names, everyone told stories.

My grandfather was the best of them, a wonderful storyteller who wove tales from Ifa with the contemporary. Not only was he a storyteller, he read widely and had a library full of rare books and literature from the Far East. It was in his library that I read my first works of speculative fiction in Yoruba. They were a series of textbooks titled *Aláwìíyé* (1-6), written by J.F. Odunjo, and the novels of D.O. Fágúnwà, which he made me read aloud because he was visually impaired. It wasn't until I turned thirteen and gained access to my brother's library of erotica that I encountered speculative fiction from the Global North.

My grandfather, like my other living ancestors, was an indulgent parent who treated us like delicate wonders of nature. So, during long holidays, we would gather around a flickering lantern, or under the cold moonlight, on mats in the compound's courtyard, to share food and, of course, tell stories.

These tales were sometimes tall, sometimes true; some were sagas that took several days of telling, while others were short and sweet. Some of these stories were retellings—edited and remixed—others were fresh off the imagination. Each story had a structure. There was the beginning, a call-and-response song in which the storyteller would call out the refrain and the audience would yell back a response to prime them for what was to come. For new stories, the first thing we had to learn were the songs so that when it was time for the call and response, you would know what to say. Then, the story itself, often interrupted by someone trying to correct the storyteller, ask a question, or just interject something silly. I remember laughter—a lot of it—and songs.

Most of these stories featured Tortoise the Cunning, Ijapa Ologbon Ewe, and its family and friends. The Ijapa I grew up with was a non-gendered being. It could time travel, live in alternate realities, or travel to other planets. Ijapa could speak a variety of languages; it also communicated easily with other life forms and extraterrestrials. Ijapa could be good or cruel, lazy or hardworking, sometimes jealous—envious even. It was hardly ever angry, because its anger moved mountains.

As a child, Ijapa was my favorite character. Even when its stories became dark and uncomfortable, I always prayed that it would survive so that it could go on to have more adventures. I saw in Ijapa all the possibilities of human flaws and perfections. Ijapa was all of us; it was none of us.

At the end of each storytelling session, the storyteller would ask what each child thought of the story. There was never a wrong answer because for all the things these stories were, not a single one of them was a morality tale. There were no good guys, no bad guys. An innocent character might end up in the gallows in one, while the criminal in the next story might just get away with it. … And often they did, for they were tales about characters living their lives on the stage of our imaginations. They were stories of the human condition.

> … So it was told that Ijapa and Yanrinbo had been living together for many years, but they had no child. They tried everything and failed. One day they were told about an Onisegun, three villages away, who was the foremost gynaecologist and pharmacologist in their district. This made them so happy they danced for joy.
>
> The following day, Ijapa and its partner, Yanrinbo,

embarked on a journey and arrived at the Onisegun's house on the evening of the following day. The Onisegun was so happy to see both of them that they were invited for the most sumptuous dinner either Ijapa or its partner had ever eaten. After eating, the Onisegun consulted Ifa on the best solution to their problems. Ifa reassured them that Ijapa and Yanrinbo would have a child but that they would need to take a medicine whose ingredients were a little difficult to find. The Onisegun said they would go and find the ingredients and that the medicine would be ready in a week. They told Ijapa that it would have to come and fetch the medicine by itself.

Ijapa eagerly returned to the Onisegun's village exactly a week later. The Onisegun handed it a fat-bottomed pot that emitted the most mouth-watering aroma. The Onisegun then warned Ijapa, sternly, not to open the pot; it must remain on its head from the beginning of the journey to the end.

So Ijapa embarked on its journey home, at first it simply enjoyed the aroma of the medicine and the warmth of the pot it was carrying on its head, but the closer Ijapa drew to the end of its journey, the curiouser—and hungrier—it became. Ijapa finally gave in to the temptation and decided to look inside the pot, "just to check" what had been teasing its senses so mercilessly. When it opened the pot, a cloud of aromas met its nose, and instead of a bunch of leaves, or roots and barks, the pot was full of a vegetable soup replete with snails, crabs, fish, beef, and pheasant ... It turned out to be one of the most delicious meals Ijapa had ever eaten.

After it was done eating, Ijapa resumed its journey—but within a few steps came the morning sickness, the next few steps were accompanied by bloating. Still Ijapa soldiered on, the now empty and cold pot on its head. It swayed from side to side as its stomach grew bigger, but walking grew difficult as its ankles began to swell.

It was when Ijapa felt the first fluttering of the baby in

its stomach that it became truly alarmed. It turned around and headed back to the Onisegun's place. A song of apology, fear, and astonishment on its lips.

CALL:	RESPONSE:
Babalawo mo wa bebe	*Alugbinrin*
Ogun to se fun mi leekan	*Alugbinrin*
To ni nmama f'owo kenu	*Alugbinrin*
To ni nmama f'ese kenu	*Alugbinrin*
Mo f'owo kan'be mo mu b'enu	*Alugbinrin*
Mo b'oju wo'kun o ri gbendu	*Alugbinrin*

And that is the end of my story.

It was during these storytelling sessions that I knew what I wanted to do with the rest of my life: Tell epic sagas of human beings being just that, human.

Ifa philosophies, arts, sciences, mathematics, poetry, metaphysics, and medicine were embedded in my first language, Yoruba. So it made absolute sense that when I started writing, I would write speculative fiction.

❦

Certain markets in certain cities are personally significant to me because important shifts in the way I see the world, in the coming and going of the people in my life, even in my body, have taken place in them. In Ifa sciences, physical marketplaces—particularly ones with T-junctions—are considered portals where beings from other realities and worlds co-mingle. I therefore approach markets with caution and respect.

One of these markets is Oja Oyingbo. Long before European imperialists named the city Lagos, Eko Akete had an Oyingbo Market, likely in the same location as it is today. Like most ancient marketplaces, Oyingbo is a free trade zone. Originally a night market where time is deep and elastic, there is absolutely nothing that can't be sold or bought in it—as long as you have your password. It is so important that there will always be commerce within its territory. And if a trader or two, or ten, decided not to participate in its commerce, their absence would go unnoticed. Oja Oyingbo thrives no matter what.

Oja Oyingbo undergirds my thoughts as I try to situate my writing career as a queer, Indigenous Yoruba, Black, feminist they/them who is vocal about racism, imperialism, and world politics while living and working in Nigeria—to varying degrees of success.

In the complex political and socioeconomic structure of the Indigenous peoples of Oduduwa, the above labels are unnecessary because all eniyan, human beings, are considered equal. The Yoruba language itself is ungendered. When I'm in this community, I have no need to identify as they/them. I don't need to state my politics as a feminist, because there's no deification of the feminine—no special category in which it could only perform certain roles. The feminine was (and still is) a visible part of the socio-political life of every compound and village; it can wield power either to benefit or to cruelty. There are no classifications meant to dehumanize or extract labor, and laws are created to protect the most vulnerable. However, each time I step out of this community into other spaces, these labels haunt me.

In 2014, former Nigerian president, Ebele Goodluck Jonathan, signed the Same Sex Marriage Prohibition bill into law. The bill had been floating around the upper and lower chambers of the Senate for nearly ten years and it effectively formalized the policing and violation of queer bodies by state and non-state actors. So, when my queer work of speculative fiction, *Adunni: The Beautiful One Has Not Yet Died*, was published by Brittle Paper to rave reviews that same year, I effectively established my writing as queer literature. And nobody in the Nigerian publishing industry would work with me.

Even before that, the literary community had never really seen me as a writer, though my children's book *Eno's Story*—published in 2010 by Cassava Republic Press—was shortlisted for the Nigerian

Prize for Literature (the NLNG Prize). Not only because of the rumors of my queerness, but because I'd never fit in.

To be seen as a writer, you have to be a member of a certain class. You have to graduate from certain universities. Because the only authors worth that name are those who have been acknowledged by Europe and America, you have to be able to hobnob with those who "own the table"—the literary agents, publishers, and magazine editors—every single one of whom is located in the Global North. The only other way of getting into this rarefied clique is by brownnosing as many established writers as possible in the fervent hope that one of them will show you the way.

I did not have the educational requirements or the class connections, so I was largely unable to access the very limited funding, residencies, travel, and opportunities afforded to Nigerian writers. Nor did I possess the niceties needed for brownnosing. The few times I was able to socialize with those who could anoint me the "next brilliant thing", my neurodivergent ass would always do or say something to turn them off.

The same year that law passed, I also completed the manuscript for my début speculative fiction novel, *Lákírí̀boto Chronicles: A Brief History of Badly Behaved Women*. It was not only queer but prominently featured Esu, one of the Irunmole of the Indigenous Peoples of Oduduwa who is often misattributed as equivalent to the devil in Christian mythology. I began sending it out to as many publishing houses as possible and got a slew of rejection emails in response.

Lákírí̀boto Chronicles would not have been the first queer novel published by a Nigerian author living in Nigeria—those would be Jude Dibia's *Unbridled* (2007) and *Blackbird* (2011). But it would have been the first queer novel of speculative fiction published by a major Nigerian publishing house. I did get one surprising acceptance from a major publishing house in 2015, but by the middle of 2016 they unceremoniously cancelled our contract.

The book wasn't published until 2018 by Booksellers Editions Africa, a small academic publishing house that did not have a publicity budget. By then, I had established myself as an advocate for queer rights and the trans community, and as an Ifa scholar. I had completely run out of social capital.

My life was not only falling apart online, it was also happening in real time. I lost my job in 2012 after leading and participating in a major anti-government protest, #OccupyNigeria. Even though I offered editorial and ghostwriting services, my finances had become precarious. It took nearly four years of futile job searches, a depression, and nearly losing my mind before I finally admitted to myself that I'd been blacklisted.

Instead of curling up and dying, as many others before me had done, I started sending out my speculative pieces to foreign online magazines. After a slew of rejections, in 2017, I finally got an acceptance—and a handsome payment—from the now-defunct *Luminous Magazine* for my short story "Phoenix," which explored witchcraft. This was followed by "The Woman with a Thousand Stars in her Hair" (*Anathema Magazine*, 2017) and "The Storm Painter" (*Strange Horizons*, 2019). In between, I wrote a collection of queer erotica for Love Africa Press in 2018.

I also focused on my second love, investigative journalism, where I thrived. Through this space, I attended workshops, accessed funding, and published important works as a neurodivergent, openly queer they/them. Was there discrimination? Did I meet bigots? Yes, many times. But because there were systems to protect people like me within that space, I was able to push back and take my stand. My self-confidence got a boost.

Between 2019 and 2020, I wrote my first science fiction novella, marrying Ifa's sciences of time travel and the mechanics of space exploration to create a post-apocalyptic landscape. I did this in response to all the science fiction books and the films I'd come across in which black bodies are rarities. In these post-apocalyptic imaginings, sexism and classicism prevailed. Even queer bodies are stereotyped and fetishized. I sent out the story and got the fastest rejection letter I've ever received. It took barely twenty-four hours. The message was loud and clear: only writers from the Global North are allowed to write science fiction, Africans should stick to fantasy.

But like Oja Oyingbo, I am here. I will occupy space, and I will continue being.

I was recently recruited by an agent; my second novel, *Swallow: Efunsetan Aniwura*, is on bookshelves nationwide; and Cipher Press, a UK-based publishing house, will be reissuing *Lakiriboto Chronicles* by summer 2023—we're in talks with another company for the audio version of the book.

I will continue writing the sciences of Ifa because that is what I am here to do. I don't need anyone to make me a seat. I came with my own table.

I am Oja Oyingbo. I will flourish, I will thrive.

Ayọ̀délé Ọlọ́fintúádé has yet to understand the concept of cis-heteronormativity. They are the author of *Swallow: Ẹfúnṣetán Aníwúrà* (2022), *Lákíríboto Chronicles: A Brief History of Badly Behaved Women* (2018), and *Eno's Story* (2010), which was shortlisted for the NLNG Prize for Literature in 2011. They are famous for being ingenious at creating chaos by merely existing. The last time they attended a literary festival they managed to spill water down an older author's dress and got themself banned for wearing too-short dresses, cut too low. Their short stories, non-fiction, research, and essays have been published in diverse international magazines and journals. They're an Ifa and Òrìsà scholar presently researching the Indigenous peoples of Yoruba and the ways their practices are intertwined with the stewardship of land and nature. And they have earned themself the cognomen of Egungun within these circles for wearing colorful socks with everything. They live in Ibadan, Nigeria, with their kids and a pair of half-wild cats.

Two Truths Means No Truths

Carlos Hernandez

The best and worst thing about growing up bilingual is that you realize how bad language is at its main job: that is, communicating.

Each language reveals the weaknesses of the other. Why are we constantly saying "I" in English? In Spanish, I don't have to say, "I am here"; I can drop the "yo" and just say "Estoy aquí." What's wrong, English-speakers? Afraid you'll wink out of existence unless you constantly assert yourself with a pronoun? Good luck with that. What a flimsy cane "I" is.

Don't laugh, Spanish. One of the reasons Spanish grammar lets you get away with dropping words is because it takes more words to say, well, pretty much everything. The Spanish language never quite got over the Baroque era: artifacts and elocutions from generations past show up in even banal sentences, dressed like the Queen of the Renaissance Faire, ready to put on a show. When I visited Mexico, Cuba, and Ecuador (to name three), I had restaurant staff who, when I thanked them, always replied, "Para servirle," "[I am] here to serve you." Yes, and I remain your most humble and obedient servant. May every planet bestow favorable omens on you, and may your humors always remain in balance, amen.

I have a theory: the lengths to which one has to go to speak Spanish may explain why it's so common to hear people reply "Sí," or "¿Cómo que no?" or "Por supuesto." "Yes," "How could it be otherwise?" "Of course,"—Spanish speakers agree with people a lot more than English speakers. Sometimes it's just easier in Spanish to agree, and then roll your eyes and do whatever the hell you want. The compactness of English, on the other hand, leads to blusterific phenomena such as, say, the House of Commons.

This is all very subjective, of course, and we can fight about it over drinks—if you're buying. But really, the subjectivity is the point. Growing up speaking both Spanish and English trained me to doubt truth-statements, since all of these truths had to be delivered by statements. Statements are made of words. And words are leaky buckets.

Or, hold on, here's a more complete metaphor: every declarative sentence asserts its veracity like the promises pro wrestlers make before a match. I remember a time when I thought professional wrestling (which I watched in English at home and in Spanish at my abuelos' and tíos' houses) was real. Oh, how I argued with my big sister about it, defending the honor of Dusty Rhodes and Ric Flair against her smug objections. Then came the disillusionment when I realized, yeah, it's all scripted. Stupid smug Maria, always being right.

But then something wonderful happened in my twenties. The love for pro wrestling returned. So what if it's scripted? Pro wrestlers are: A) incredible athletes; B) devoted to their craft to the extreme (see secret razor blades tucked into waistbands for sudden and 100% real blood); C) method actors par excellence who are utterly devoted to "kayfabe" (i.e., staying in character so hard fans never catch a glimpse of the complex, nuanced human being who's playing the face or the heel). They create momentous battles with larger-than-life characters that combine the excesses of cartoons with real, high-flying bodies. I couldn't have finished my PhD in Literature if I didn't love epic shit like that.

All language is kayfabe. With bravura and splendor, with its oiled muscles and spangled masks, it screams into the mic and assures us all that justice will be served. I couldn't have articulated that as a kid, not in those terms, but I knew it. I lived it. I loved stories, but not because they were "true" or full of useful "morals." I loved stories because they seemed more full of life than life.

That's the job of all language, in the end: to pass on to the listener a lot of life in a short amount of time. Language is dense with happenings. Events, personalities, mysteries, consequences, opinions—language delivers a heaping helping of the mess of existence in every sentence.

Let's do an experiment. Put this essay on your lap or look away from your screen for ten seconds. The experiment works best if you're alone. Look at the ceiling or sky, and listen hard. Count to ten, and then come back to this essay.

Welcome back. Did you feel, in those seconds, how diffuse life felt, how gentle and quiet and slow? No, you didn't, not if you have kids or pets, not if your spouse wanted to know where you put the pickles, not if anything interfered with you just sitting quietly and letting the world come to you through your senses. I am interfering right now, with my sentences, in fact. These sentences are rushing information to you word by word. They're thick with connotations and urgent rhetoric. They make you think.

That's true even if you think I'm full of shit. Whether or not you agree, you have to decide if you agree. You've still got to do all the sorting out and fact-checking with language, just as you do in your own life. But you get a lot of life, quickly, and that's what matters. Over time, if you're good at separating valid and sound ideas from hokum, you'll net more of the useful and beautiful stuff.

But either way, you'll get more of life's life. And that has value, too.

I had two First Communions. One in English, one in Spanish.

My English First Communion was my "vanilla" sacrament. Everything went as it should. No surprises. I was "trained" in my CCD classes, sure, but the training was so easy, even the A students started cutting up in class. I remember one kid made a massive paper airplane out of a newspaper and flew it in class. The nun teaching us was writing something on the board when he launched it, but she sensed something and turned around just in time to see its inaugural flight. It flew surprisingly well, considering the flimsiness of newspaper. Her face fell as she watched its slow, crane-like flight. You could see in her expression that she thought she was failing us. She was a sweet, nice person. I still feel bad about that airplane.

That was the most dramatic event I can remember from my English First Communion. Everything else was low-key, easy, in and out. I wore jeans and a T-shirt the day of. Father Gerry, pastor, gave me my first Communion wafer himself. He was also the priest who took my First Confession. I was in fourth grade, but he was already admonishing me not to masturbate. I wasn't masturbating at that age and just thought it was hilarious that people did that. When I got older, I ignored the hell out of Father Gerry's admonitions and masturbated like the primate I am.

That's what Catholic sacraments in English meant to me: they were well-meaning and easy to understand, but out of touch, and maybe not all that applicable to my life.

By way of contrast, during my Spanish First Communion, I saw a miracle.

I don't say this lightly. I don't believe in miracles, haven't for a long, long time. But I witnessed one, during my Spanish First Communion. It is as undeniable as other fundamental childhood memories I have. Thank goodness for my studies in literature, which have taught me all about unreliable narrators and the fallibility of memory, all about the way our thinking swerves sometimes toward the magical! Sometimes you tell a story enough times, the way you tell it becomes the memory, and all that's left of the truth is kayfabe. Sweet, delicious kayfabe.

Here's the thing: as I sit here, recalling the story in preparation of writing it down for you, I can feel the reality of it in my chest. I don't *believe* it. But its truth continues to assert itself inside of me, in spite of me.

To set the scene: imagine young Carlos, standing at the far end of the aisle at Saint Martha's Catholic Church, where they gave a Spanish Mass at 12:30 p.m. on Sundays. Carlos is not wearing jeans and a T-shirt, as he did for his English First Communion. Despite the Florida humidity, he is wearing a three-piece suit as white as a saint's beard. There are cloth crosses on his shoulders, almost epaulettes, white and trimmed in golden thread. The outfit's completed by brand-new dress shoes, white and tight and laceless.

Carlos is, in short, the very picture of a snappily dressed young prophet, dressed exactly the way his mami pictures him, imagines his future.

(You see, when Mami was pregnant with me, she fell. She was terrified she was going to lose me, just as she had lost the pregnancy before the one that yielded me. So, she prayed to God and said that, if He permitted me to live, my life would be dedicated to His Glory. No wonder her favorite picture of me had always been my First Communion picture. I don't think she ever moved past that image of me in her mind.)

Carlos is standing with another boy, whom I won't name. But he is similarly dressed. He was not, however, trained for Spanish First Communion the way young Carlos was. Carlos was trained by his abuela, Papi's mami, whom everyone called Ramona. Abuela Ramona was a santera, a religion that Carlos's mami equated with witchcraft. Even knowing that, you can't imagine how terribly the two got along. In retrospect, it's incredible to me that Abuela was entrusted with preparing me for Spanish First Communion. Mami and Papi must have had tons of their patented horrible fights over it.

There's Abuela Ramona now, sitting in a pew with Abuelo Leopoldo, one pew back from the rest of the family. As I pass her, she looks at me, but with her usual, sphinx-like inscrutability. No smile or encouragement or criticism. She's just looking. It's the same look, mind you, that Mami sometimes thought could deliver the Evil Eye. Ask my sisters and you'll hear that Abuela had a powerful Evil Eye. Once, she complimented my little sister Barbara, and poor Barbara fell sick for a week, until Mami enlisted her friend Vicky, who knew of these things, to help her break the spell.

(All this has to be bullshit. But also, it all happened, and it feels as real to me as my name.)

Anyway, the good news is that for whatever reason, I have always been immune to Ramona's Evil Eye and could return her gaze with no ill effects.

The most important thing about Communion, according to Ramona, was to always treat it as a holy event. Every time you took Communion, you were experiencing a miracle. The wafer in your mouth would transform, literally, into the body and blood of Jesus, who is God. Act, therefore, with solemnity. You do not chew God! Let the wafer dissolve on your tongue. Keep your mouth shut and your head bowed, and think about the fact that God's body is joining your body in that miraculous moment.

You do not chew God! That point was driven home hard. When I asked why, I would get flowery explanations, but really, it just seemed like the most important part of the whole sacrament was to not treat the Body of Christ like Bubble Yum.

Easy enough. I and the other boy reached the altar, and the priest gave me Communion first, placing the wafer on my tongue. I took it carefully into my mouth and patiently waited for it to dissolve.

Meanwhile, the other boy—remember, he had no Abuela Ramona to prepare him—took Communion. But he didn't know not to chew. He chewed the wafer like he was gnawing on beef jerky, with his mouth open, and kind of smiling.

And his mouth filled with blood.

Not a little. A lot of blood. The bits of wafer were roiling around in it, like rafts in a merciless red ocean. Most of the miracle, in fact, is that none of the blood spilled out of his mouth. There was a solid mouthful of blood, half-submerging his baleen-whale tongue.

This isn't a dream I had about First Communion, before or after the fact. I know this because, at that moment, I turned to look at Abuela Ramona, and she did not return her normal, impassive, implacable gaze. She tilted her head and flicked her eyebrows. Her body language could not be clearer. *See? That's why you don't chew the Host.*

Years later, as a teenager, I asked her about it, and she remembered the blood in the boy's mouth as perfectly as I did. Whatever actually happened, it was something that was witnessable by two people.

So, what did happen? How do I, now a skeptic, a person who doesn't believe in miracles, explain this? I have theories. Maybe the boy bit his cheek. Maybe he'd been eating a cherry candy right before Communion (though you're not supposed to eat for an hour beforehand; he should have known!). I used to, and still get, bloody noses for no good reason; maybe he did, too. Maybe, maybe, maybe.

I have no evidence. This happened more than forty years ago, and my star witness, Abuela Ramona, santera and wielder of a mighty Evil Eye, has died. The case will remain forever cold. All I can tell you is that, right now, as I write this, I can picture the boy's chewing face, and see the blood and wafer tumbling in his mouth, and that I was not the only witness. Its undeniability, and the distrust and disbelief I have of my memory, are both forever part of this story.

In terms of communicating any kind of truth to you, my two First Communions are pretty much a bust. But in terms of what it means to be tightrope-walking between cultures, and the vantage that you get of the world when you're up that high, with everything literally on the line? I've got something better than the truth to share with you. I have a story.

New York Times bestselling author **Carlos Hernandez** is the author of *Sal and Gabi Break the Universe,* for which he won the Pura Belpré Award in 2020, *Sal and Gabi Fix the Universe, The Assimilated Cuban's Guide to Quantum Santeria,* and numerous short stories and poems, almost always with a speculative bent. By day, Carlos is a CUNY Professor of English, as well as a game designer and enthusiast. Look for him on socials: @writeteachplay.

Messy
A Letter to My Editor

Chịkọdịlị Emelụmadụ

D ear Chinelo,

Forgive my tardiness. I'm aware it has been nearly nine months since I was meant to reply and although you have been busy yourself with editing duties and new arrivals, I really should have said something and not allowed you to chase me.

The truth is, I find myself in a bit of a bind without certainty as to what is binding me. I've wondered if I have some form of the dreaded "pandemic brain." Yet I've produced work—slowly, sparsely—but I have done, yes. Not to mention working on my debut novel, *Dazzling*, selling it, prepping it for publication, and so on. I can only conclude that my reticence to contribute to this anthology stems from the subject. I do so loathe telling people what to do.

That's a lie. I actually like telling people what to do. Sometimes. When I can bestir myself.

I am aware however, of the very individual nature of writing. There are many paths, many avenues. Many pitfalls. Who am I to advise anyone on anything? Knowing what I know now, I should have simply married rich while my breasts were still in their original position … you know, standing up.

Instead, I married for "love" and cut my craft teeth while juggling a newborn and keeping home for a spouse who traveled for his own career even as I waited for my turn to shine. Then I went mad, cut my hair, suffered from depression, went on medication, worked odd hours, slept little, had another child to keep the first one company, suffered betrayal, died, was buried, and ... Here. We. Are.

Here we fucking are.

❦

I can tell you stories of what it means to be a woman shoehorning herself into a life that does not nurture her. I could talk about the 4:30 a.m. calls from my father, who chose those times because he felt that whatever guard I had would be down. The "What are you doing with your life?" interrogations when I was twenty-two years old, and again at twenty-three, and again at twenty-four.

Or should I talk about the respectable jobs I worked at simply to be allowed to exist while practising my art in secret? What of the non-respectable gigs: Data Inputter; Warm Office Body Number One; Seat Warmer; Shit Taker, all shouldered for the "respectability" of earning something—anything—while writing on napkins, paper scraps, and skin during my breaks? Jobs with small money and even smaller prospects? The feeling of cheap Primark shirts tight around the arms and shoulders with buttons gaping across your breasts, the feeling of being misplaced—mislaid—in your own life?

No, that's too dark.

I shall talk instead of landing that one big job with an international broadcaster, the lightness around your shoulders that comes from having your parents hear your voice two, three times a week. No more 4:00 a.m. calls. No more "what-are-you-doing-with-your-life-maybe-you-should-do-a-PhD."

But there was still the "where is the man?" waiting. Then, finally, the man. The man! One thinks, "At least he will never force me to be who I am not," and "At least I can pursue my real ambition." And one marries him because what is more respectable for African parents than marriage? And for a while there is peace in the land. Right?

Wrong.

I made the sacrifice to stay at home and raise my first child. He has many allergies and is prone to anaphylaxis. Before we found out why he was losing so much weight, I would cook three to four meals a day, trying to tempt his appetite. I taught him his letters, numbers, and writing—by the time he started school he was miles ahead. I taught him to ride a bike and a scooter. I suffered insomnia, so at night, I worked on my short stories.

Morning would meet me typing away. Then, I would tuck the laptop under my armchair before leaping up to prepare breakfast and pack for a whole day of activities outside the house—all while my partner slept. (The tedium of mother-baby groups! I'd rather stick a hot butter knife in my eye than do those again!) Home for a nap in the afternoon—his, mine—then more learning, more play, laundry, dinner, bathtime, bedtime, cleaning, middle-of-the-night waking, middle-of-the-night putting back to bed, then click-clacking eight, ten stories a week, before starting again the next day.

I poured all I was into my family and my craft until I had nothing left. The stories had to come from me so the voices followed me wherever I went. Reams of dialogue, whole paragraphs of worldbuilding, came to me in inopportune moments: the shower, church, while trying to stop a wriggling baby from falling off the changing table with a shitty nappy in one hand and a face full of hot pee. I grabbed minutes by the fistful, writing everywhere.

But the early morning calls didn't stop. Now, it was to ask when I was going back to work. I was the big broadcaster, but they no longer heard my voice on the airwaves—and neither did their friends. What was I doing? What the hell is *writing*? Unrealistic. I was wasting my Master's. Go for a PhD. What did I mean, *what for*? For the life of a "doctor-of-something." Much more profitable. Much more secure.

I can't tell you much, but I can tell you how much unbelief— mine, others, mine fed by others—aches. It's worse when you hear reports that, upon being asked about your well-being, your father had replied: "She is just a housewife."

The thing about being told that your existence is invalid until you prove your worth is that you begin to believe it. And when you look for support and continuously meet turned backs, a heat begins to bloom in your chest, then tighten, and spread.

IT HURTS.

The things my dad said to me ... I came to realize that how he saw himself in society mattered more than my welfare. I understand now that with the way he was raised, he has a face he must show the world, but at the time, I saw that I was more or less alone. I recognized that this is how people die, trying to remain respectable, trying to please their parents.

So maybe, if I was to give advice, it would be this: You have to be okay with being the only person who believes in you. If other people do, great. But if they do not, you cannot let yourself be torn up by it. It is very difficult and takes some doing, but it is not impossible.

⁕

Two years after my father made the "housewife" comment, I was nominated for The Caine Prize for African Writing, one of the continent's most prestigious literary awards, for an original short story. But by that point, I'd stopped caring so much about prizes. I found that doing the work—the reading, the writing— was much more fulfilling.

Recently, my father visited. I had just sold my first novel, Dazzling, and, true to African parent form, he wanted to know how much it had fetched. I told him. He converted it to Naira and his eyes fell out of his head.

"Goodness knows what that [Chimamanda Ngozi] Adichie girl makes then," he exclaimed. "She must be carrying it home in trailers!"

I shrugged, allowed myself a little smirk, and carried on housewifely.

Our parents admire writers like Chinua Achebe and Wole Soyinka and Buchi Emecheta and Flora Nwapa from afar but are either unwilling or unable to understand the rigors that brought them their fame and—some—fortune. I can empathize.

A good number of our parents had parents who witnessed the arrival of the first Christian missionaries. Our parents watched as their old order was overturned and a new one took its place. They reaped the benefits of a Western education that took them far and wide, farther than their parents could ever imagine. I understand that, for them, the idea of failing in this new world cannot bear thinking about. Hence the myriad degrees. Hence the constant push for bigger and brighter and better. They drive us towards careers in which there is longevity and certainty: medicine, law, engineering. People will always get sick. People will always need arbitration. And in an expanding world, we will always need to build.

I empathize, but it does not mean that I don't loathe the system with every fibre of my being.

A year after our conversation about my novel, I handed my father a copy of the anthology *Of This Our Country*, a collection of personal essays by twenty-four Nigerian writers, including me. He broke into prayer. He poured a libation and prayed ofo, then told me that I had fulfilled the name his own father gave me decades ago. I'm choosing to keep it within me for now, but it translates to "One that cuts a path (where once there was nothing)." Apparently, my father refused to give me the name at the time because he felt it was not modern enough. But he admitted, almost tearing up, that I embodied it, that he has been watching me forge my own path all this while—no matter what anyone says.

So, why the fight? Fear, my friend. Fear, for in Igboland a child is an extension of her people. And I broke the rules. I broke the rules by insisting on my own unmapped, uncertain way.

Today, when I stand, there are people who stand with me. I am grateful for their support, their aid, their succor. Igbo people say, "When something stands, something else stands next to it," and I hope I can be an embodiment for other storytellers out there. It is comforting to have a tribe, and to finally count my beloved parents among their number.

In every way, I choose to remain free, to follow my path. As I was named, so am I.

Best wishes,

Chịkọdịlị.

Chikọdịlị Emelụmadụ was born in Worksop, Nottinghamshire, and happily raised in Awka, Nigeria. Her work has been shortlisted for the Shirley Jackson Award (2015) and The Caine Prize for African Literature (2017 & 2020) and has won a Nommo Award (2020).

In 2019, she emerged winner of the inaugural Curtis Brown First Novel prize for her manuscript *Dazzling*. Her debut novel by the same name will be published in February 2023 and is now available for preorder.

She tweets as @chemelumadu.

Small Awakenings

Dominique Dickey

I wanted to be a writer before I knew how to write.

Before I could pick up a pencil, I knew I wanted to tell stories, and that I wanted those stories to be printed on paper for people to read. Some of my earliest memories are of dictating words to my mother and grandmother, who would write them down for me.

When I was four years old, I decided I wanted to "write" a scary story like the horror movies I was barred from watching even though their trailers captivated me. I dictated the opening scene to my mom, then became inconsolably frightened until she changed the ending. She finished the story for me, making it toothless. She made the blood fake.

But she couldn't take away the fact that I'd terrified myself with my own imagination. That moment, weeping at the kitchen table over the unknown fate of a protagonist I'd invented and put through hell, quite literally changed my life. I'd transformed my own emotional state with my words alone; it was then that I was truly hooked.

I'm aware that this makes me very lucky: it's pure luck to find the thing that makes you impossibly, incandescently happy—and to have found it at such a young age—and then get to spend the rest of your life honing that skillset. I'm very grateful for how it all worked out. But I digress.

I started writing because, quite simply, I couldn't imagine a life spent doing anything else, because writing is where I go to feel alive. I kept writing—even through the growing pains that come with honing one's craft—because it keeps me sane. The act of writing, whether I'm dictating or holding a pen or tapping away at a keyboard, has always been compulsive. I often feel like I'm being dragged along behind my own creativity—like I have no choice but to show up to the blank page and see what new magic I can make.

But learning to write was only half the battle; the other half was learning to write freely. I still had to learn to write like *myself*.

When I first started writing, I wrote along the lines of what I read or what I saw on television—remember, my first attempt to write horror came from the appeal of movies I was only allowed to watch in small bites. I don't think this experience is at all unique in writing or in any other creative art. You learn to play guitar by playing covers. You find your own music by playing someone else's first.

I wrote what I read: what my peers recommended, what was assigned to me at school, what was promoted at Borders Bookstore or at the local library. I wanted so badly to live inside of these stories, and writing was my way in. I wrote about the lives I felt I was missing out on, because these were what I saw modeled for me in fiction—idealized selves that I first stepped into as a reader.

Most of the protagonists I read about were white, cis, and straight. Does it surprise anyone that my idealized selves were also white? Through my characters—characters who fit the mold of Western fiction—I could shake off the feeling that something was wrong with me. Becoming them, if only for a time, made me feel like the world valued me. My bookshelves were colonized and so was my imagination.

To her credit, my mother offered me stories that showed that there were other lives worth dreaming about. But I rejected them in favor of keeping up with what my (white, cis, straight) peers were reading. I wanted to read about adventure (white people going on adventures) and romance (straight people falling in love) and imagined worlds (populated almost solely by cis people). When I look back at my earliest work, my heart aches for that kid. The stories I wrote, while upbeat on the surface, were laced with such unhappiness. I wrote because I wanted to be anyone but myself—and I'm so happy I'm not in that place anymore.

There was no one moment that woke me up, but a series of small awakenings.

The first was when I was in middle school. I wrote a story set in Memphis in 1963 and thought myself clever because, as a way to point out the time and location to the reader, I had a character comment on a news headline of the assassination of Dr. Martin Luther King, Jr. When my mother read the piece, she was appalled.

"You write like a white person," she said. What she meant was that I wasn't just writing white, cishet characters; I was writing with white, cishet sensibilities.

For example, I often didn't specify my characters' race because I'd defaulted to writing about white people, and I'd learned that a lack of specificity always meant whiteness. It was in this moment, sitting in the car with my mom, that I realized that I'm not afforded that same set of assumptions. My race is always specified. It's the first thing people see when they look at me—and it should be among the first things observed about my characters.

But altering a character's race changes them on a far deeper level than just their appearance. It changes how they think and how they interact with the world around them. No Black narrator in 1963 would remark on Dr. Martin Luther King, Jr.'s assassination over their morning coffee like it didn't matter. For a Black narrator, that would be the *entire* conversation.

"You have to show them who you are," my mother said. I had to write from my own experience. To stop running from who I was, using writing as an escape into an impossible dream. I was never going to be white or cis or straight, so I gained nothing by pining for that life. I had to put myself on the page, holding back nothing.

After that first awakening, it's safe to say that I stopped trying to be someone I wasn't. Translating that change to my work was much harder.

So, I kept writing the same derivative, dishonest work I'd been writing all along—not because I wanted to imagine a more normative life for myself, but because I was afraid of revealing my inner truths. I was afraid that I would give away too much of myself and face a kind of rejection that my psyche would never recover from.

Writing characters who share facets of my identity entails a deep vulnerability. Every queer Black character I put to paper still feels like unzipping my skin and spilling out my insides. Bits of me exist in my characters, which means that a rejection of those characters can feel like rejection of my entire self. Because, unlike fictional characters, I can't be broken into my component parts.

The next of my small awakenings occurred when I was applying for college, a process that forced me to be honest about myself in a way I'd seldom been in other contexts. Strangers were going to look at my applications and judge me—quite literally deciding whether or not I was worthy. This was it: the kind of rejection I'd spent years running from.

I applied to a handful of schools, writing essays that contextualized my faltering academic performance with truths about my mental health and family life that I was reluctant to share with even my closest friends. I got a few acceptances and a few rejections.

And the rejections didn't break me.

I learned what it meant to tell a stranger who I was and have them respond with a frosty "no, thanks." I learned to be resilient in the face of that discomfort. Not everyone is going to love me, but I can't give them a chance to if I don't show up as myself.

I got a BA in creative writing in a program that leaned on the workshop model. Students present their work to their peers with no accompanying commentary, then are expected to sit silently while their classmates discuss what they perceive as the piece's strengths and weaknesses. Because the writer is not able to offer any context or steer the discussion, feedback often focuses on bending the presented work to the readers' aesthetic sensibilities, rather than heightening aspects of the work that the writer already loves.

Four years of this both threatened and reinforced my newfound imaginative freedom. My classmates' notes, well-intentioned as they were, revolved around the white cishet worldview I'd spent ages trying to claw my way out of. Their feedback revealed more about their own aesthetics than it did about my strengths and weaknesses as a writer.

Would it have been easier—and wouldn't I have made better grades—if I'd just given in and written the kind of work my classmates and professors expected to see? Maybe. But not every story lands for every reader because not every story is *for* every reader.

Just as I was given feedback, I was given the opportunity to offer it. For every story that I presented, I was expected to read and critique fifteen others which were written by a largely homogeneous group. Seeing the same characters and tropes over and over again was another small awakening: by articulating what worked and what missed the mark in my classmates' stories, I learned what I like and what I don't. I learned what I want to emulate as a writer, what makes me fall in love as a reader, and what I'd rather steer clear of. For me, these lessons were the one saving grace of the workshop model, which frequently fails marginalized students.[1]

Speculative fiction writers have the freedom to imagine *anything*, and I believe that this comes with the responsibility to question hegemonic systems and imagine alternatives. The systems I challenge in my fiction have direct bearing on my life, but I had to free my own imagination before I could depict these new pathways in my work. I'm writing stories I want to read, stories I wish I could have read sooner. I want them to be a life raft, or a skeleton key, or a guiding star. I want my stories to be a tool that others can use to get free.

I'm still waking up, but I'm happy with where I am now. I no longer write to forget the contours of my experience—I know who I am as a writer, and I know *who* I write for. Most days, writing still feels compulsive, and I still leave everything I have on the page. I hope that lasts for a long time. Even more fervently, I hope the small awakenings keep coming.

---

1. For further discussion of the workshop model's flaws, as well as several proposed alternative pedagogies, I encourage you to refer to *Craft in the Real World* by Matthew Salesses.

Dominique Dickey is a writer, editor, cultural consultant, and Nebula Award-winning RPG hooligan. In addition to creating TRIAL, a narrative courtroom tabletop role-playing game about race in the criminal justice system, and co-creating *Tomorrow on Revelation III*, a tabletop role-playing game about surviving and building community on a hyper-capitalist space station, Dominique has written for *Thirsty Sword Lesbians, Dungeons & Dragons,* and *Pathfinder*. Their fiction has appeared in *Anathema Magazine, Fantasy Magazine,* and *Lightspeed Magazine,* among other venues. Dominique works as a designer and editor at Monte Cook Games. They live in the DC area, and are always on the hunt for their next idea. You can keep in touch at dominiquedickey.com.

No Net Below
The Lure of Speculative Fiction

Hannah Onoguwe

Many of my fondest childhood memories are rooted in Jos. This melting pot of cultures and religions in the Nigerian Middle Belt was famous for its conducive weather and the many foreigners who lived there. We moved to Jos from Ibadan when I was four years old. It was in grade school there that the most important friendships in my life budded, and where I began writing and discovered my love for it.

In those days, my friends and I all wrote. We would exchange notebooks filled with fictional preteen and high school angst and encourage or threaten each other to finish those stories. My father would take my scribblings and ask his secretary to type them up. I even had an article published in my church magazine. In secondary school, my new friends would pass around a notebook featuring my current story, eager for the next installment.

I went back to Ibadan for university, where I continued writing occasionally, but returned to Jos when I got my present job as a liaison between a software company and the Nigeria Immigration Service. I left Jos in 2014 when my job transferred me to Yenagoa, but I am always stoked to return to its don't-I-know-you neighborhood vibe, the familiarity of freezing mornings, and the joy of reliable suya.

During my time in Jos, my writing and I lived a charmed existence, mostly getting along with each other, and basking in the praise and approval of friends, family, and teachers. So, I was quite unprepared to hear a dissenting opinion. One day at the office, as some of us talked about writers in general and Nigerian writers in particular, it seemed natural for me to casually confess that I was a writer myself. Everyone made polite noises of surprise or admiration—except for one officer who stared at me in disbelief.

"You, a writer?" he scoffed with hand gestures, aiming, I think, to cut me down to size. "How many books you don write? Who know your name, sef?"

I was taken aback. I mean, mouth hanging open and everything. He and I had always gotten along, and I would have gone so far as to say we were friends of a sort. We shared a workspace, and our conversations up to this point had been conducted with mutual respect and gentle ribbing. In fact, he still calls me every once in a long while to find out how I am doing.

That day, in that moment, the confidence in my art which I had taken for granted began, alarmingly, to fragment. But I forced myself to recover quickly, refusing to be crushed by his attitude. Outside of our work environment, we had little to nothing in common—not a love for words nor, obviously, a consideration for tact. I was more disappointed to discover he was the type to put someone down without asking questions, without taking the trouble to get more information, without a cursory effort to be kind. I knew he would not attempt to read anything I'd written—he did not even respect the fact that I had.

That day at the office is forever impressed on my memory as a reminder that there are those who, on hearing something about you they know little about or understand, will decide it is their moral duty to "wake" you up from unrealistic dreams, to yank you back to earth by telling you what they think is the unvarnished truth. Or those who, maybe, just take pleasure in being nasty.

That experience was excellent training for when, years later, I would ask the writer of a popular blog at the time to read my collection of short romantic stories and write a review of it. Barely a day later, she sent an email apologizing that she could not get into it as it did not "kindle" her interest. Talk about my writing career sinking before ever leaving the shore! These instances helped to teach me not to put much stock in other people's opinions. Some people won't get why I bother writing, others will only see it as a nice hobby.

✧

On the other end of the spectrum are those who expect that if we aren't changing the world with our writing, then we haven't begun. It is a burden often placed on women writers. A burden weighing even heavier on Black women. On Black African women from "third-world" countries where the governments are steeped in patriarchy, not-quite-liberated from military rule, partial to ass-kissers. On Black African women who dare define themselves as feminist. Oh, and are those women married? With children? Still married? They haven't been pursued out of their homes by husbands who have had enough? Then that female Black African feminist wife mama is not telling the truth. Because to have a happy African home, you cannot be a feminist.

I must confess: while I am a feminist all the time, I am also an unquestioning African woman—much of the time. This means one who often defers to her husband, who smiles demurely when family makes certain assumptions, who automatically tucks sacrifice around her like a boubou—familiar, comfortable, voluminous—without being asked.

More often than not, African writers are enjoined to use their craft as an opportunity to speak truth to power, to wield "the pen as a sword" and ceaselessly be the voice of the voiceless, the defender of the oppressed. If we dare to indulge in writing about unrealistic, frivolous themes, we are treating this gift as something common and not taking the high calling of standing in the gap for our nation, of being the last bastion of hope seriously enough. Granted, these weightier themes are important and, in many cases, necessary. But how about African writers just being allowed to define their writing for themselves?

About two years or so ago, a writers' organization in Nigeria, of which I am a member, marked a major anniversary. They organized an event which included a panel discussion on new writing and the importance of standards. One of the discussants, someone I respect, said that he thought high-quality writing had to be "believable" and "based on reality." The former I totally agreed with, but I was a bit disappointed at the latter. Regardless of genre, it is the author's responsibility to make a story believable. But if everything every writer wrote was based on reality, how dull, how limiting would the world be? How undertaxed our imaginations? Without witches and juju, dragons and bush babies, edible houses and talking beasts, how devoid of sparkle would our stories be?

Besides, on this side of the Sahara, juju is not fiction. We take in stories of witchcraft and questionable supernatural happenings with our meals and pass them around like kilishi in the workplace. Doctors will take patients aside after routine consultations and advise them to seek "spiritual" solutions, morgue attendants report matter-of-factly about how they often have to shout at their "inmates" to keep their noise down, to stop singing, or to return from their nocturnal visits on time. Unsolicited, friends, family members—even random acquaintances—will recount dreams they had about you, fully expecting you to take seriously what those visions reveal. We might raise our brows at the details, but we rarely question the storyteller's earnestness, or their sanity. It has been our way; it is our way.

In Nigeria, when you come across something that boggles the mind, rest assured that it won't make any more sense upon deeper inspection. These are stories that lack a single thread of logic that would fasten their seams together. Stories that do not seek rational explanations. Like the story of a certain girl in Lagos who wanted to get married and traveled out of town to consult with a seer. The seer warned her to be wary of her boyfriend. By the time she got back, said boyfriend was livid: "You went to ask about me, abi? You don't know what you're dealing with!" And he threw her out of the house. How could he have possibly known what she had spoken with the seer about? Exactly.

Or how about the story of siblings who lost their mother, and after finding out that she had practiced black magic and harmful juju while alive, obstinately refused to bury her in the designated place prescribed by the funeral processes of their community? Due to this infraction, the firstborn began to slowly go mad and—because his siblings further neglected to take the recommended actions, despite varied and urgent advisors— deteriorated until he died.

There are stories.

I often muse that I could never run out of inspiration even if I tried. But as a true African, I would be lying if I said I don't worry about stepping on any toes, physical or otherworldly. You don't want to misrepresent or offend anyone, human or nonhuman. And though you might want to be original as a writer, creatively bending and twisting what you know, in Nigeria it is likely you might stumble across a rendition of similar events that reveals that real life wore it better.

Yet, the first speculative fiction story I attempted to write was a work of "hard" science fiction. It was for the *Imagine Africa 500* anthology edited by Billy Kahora whose theme required reimagining the continent 500 years into the future. Until then, I'd only written romances. I had devoured tons of romance novels growing up, as many young girls—and just as many young boys— do, so it was only natural to begin my writing journey there. Writing speculative fiction for me was a chance to break the monotony and challenge myself not to consider a happy ending, addictive though such might be.

Whenever I saw calls for submissions for "hard" science fiction, I would usually walk on by, and not just because mathematics and I have always been at odds. In my head, science fiction is formulaic and often so steeped in process that whenever I attempt to read it, my whole physiology undergoes a subtle but telling change: I throw my shoulders back, purse my lips, and reset my brain for what it is about to receive. It is a maze rife with fine details, beset by prickly obstacles made of indecipherable terminologies on a mission to lacerate me. My heart curls in a particular dread when I hear the word "Afrofuturism." I'm not quite sure what's expected of me or my writing. It's empowering, no doubt, to imagine a future that holds more agency than we Africans might possess at the moment. But sometimes I fear even my writer's imagination is too limited to envision it. Too often the present, especially what is familiar and recurring in our politics, weighs me down so that my creativity is handicapped and cannot take flight.

So, that story became more an exploration about the lengths a mother might go to protect her relationship with her child and keep her secrets from coming to light. I tried to infuse it with authenticity, and—admittedly—elements of wishful thinking around what future scientific studies might reveal to humankind by that time.

Enter the Climate Imagination Fellowship with the Center for Science and the Imagination, an awesome opportunity for me to write stories about climate change and climate action—stories based on real science. The plus was that I wasn't going to have to do much theorizing. I would be talking to researchers, policymakers, and scientists, fashioning my story around what I gleaned from them. However, even that one job began to grow tentacles that mired me in self-doubt: Am I asking the right questions? Do I sound like I know what I am talking about? Is my story science fiction-y enough?

As I educate myself more, though, I realize that I might be allowing myself to fall into a neo-colonialist trap where my roles and abilities and indeed, my permissions, are set by the West. It was American author Norman Spinrad who asserted in *Asimov's* magazine in 2010 that "third world cultures have no conception of the future," something Indian science fiction writer and physicist Vandana Singh thoroughly debunked in an essay titled "Alternate Visions: Some Musings on Diversity in SF" on her blog *Antariksh Yatra*. She said that "just like anywhere else, people in the third world do think about the future" and that "science fiction isn't necessarily *about* the future" (emphasis mine).

Science fiction is changing; character development and dialogue don't have to suffer at the expense of scientific jargon, and more expansive vistas are opening up and being tapped into.

Since then—as I tend to pen character-driven stories over plot-driven ones—I've stumbled across more accommodating spots in the genre for my writing, places where I can sit cross-legged with my laptop and share comfortable company.

⌘

I often have difficulty pegging where my speculative fiction belongs. Some are science fiction, yes, though far more of the tapioca pudding variety than the fufu. Others contain fantastical elements, though not enough to be considered fantasy—just liberal portions of the weird and not-quite-normal. Mostly, they're magical realism, as I often source inspiration from the "stranger than fiction" things we hear about in my corner of the world.

As a mother, I find a number of my stories speak to my fears for or about my children. There was "Remember," published in Issue 23 of *Eleven Eleven: A Journal of Literature and Art* in 2017. In it, a seven or eight-month-old (an unlikely narrator, as one would-be editor explained in their rejection) observes her parents quarrel over the role of a certain female in her father's life and ends up being abducted from her crèche by the scorned woman. The story was sparked by a comment my sister-in-law made one day about my first child, who was a baby at the time: "If someone kidnaps him now, that means he won't remember anything," she had said. To which my husband too-readily replied, "No. No, he won't." While part of me recognized that the conversation was mere theory about a baby's developmental limitations, the bigger part was speechless with horror, biting back knee-jerk retorts. Mentally, in pure Nigerian Pentecostal style, I doused my infant with the blood of Jesus to cancel even the conception of any such tragedy—just in case.

When I eventually shared the draft of that story with my husband, his first comment was about the other woman who had sparked the fight between the couple. It was a page I'd shamelessly torn from his life experience: a female acquaintance of his, frustrated with being single and with no relationship prospects in sight, had once propositioned that he father a child with her in the old fashioned way. When he told me of the incident—long after it happened, as men are wont to do—I smirked. While I could sympathize with his friend over the pressures our society mounts on single women, I couldn't abide the fact that, at the time she had suggested this, she was aware that he was engaged to me. Or that I wasn't armed with this information on the couple of occasions I had been pleasant to her.

Then there's "Old Photographs," my story published in *Omenana Magazine* in 2017, about a woman who has taken certain actions to keep her daughter's father away from them. As we progress, we see her reticence about the situation backfire as it only stokes the young girl's curiosity, unwittingly drawing them both into near-fatal danger. That feeling of helplessness, of being unable to guard your child from every threat, especially as they get older, is evident in the story. In much of my writing, I force myself to face my fears, probable or real. Hopefully, knock on wood, living them out speculatively in an alternate universe will ensure it doesn't happen in this one.

I have lived other emotional issues through my stories as well. When a close in-law suddenly passed on some years ago, I imagined him meeting my long-departed mother in the afterlife, sharing conversations and trading parenting experiences. Thus was the story "Yellow Means Stay" birthed. In 2020 it was shortlisted for the Afritondo Short Story Prize and published in an anthology of short stories of the same name. At first, it was a way to work out my grief and somehow keep my loved ones close. As stories tend to do, it morphed into something different from what I had initially envisaged and ended up as a love story. But its origins will never be forgotten, nor will, I imagine, the people who inspired it.

So, yes, I work out my sundry issues with my keyboard. Putting them into my stories and revisiting it all in the editing and re-editing process somehow serves as a kind of therapy so that in the long run I can look back at those situations with humor. Sometimes.

Recently, in a mentoring opportunity for the 2022 graduating class of my secondary school alma mater, I mentioned how writing can be great for the culture and is often its own reward. But I also warned that if you pursue it as a career, putting in the sweat to improve your art and eke out words people find publishable, then monetary compensation should eventually be part of that process.

When I was interviewed by Geoff Ryman for his series of articles "100 African Speculative Fiction Writers" in *Strange Horizons* magazine, I remember him asking if I was writing speculative fiction because of the money. At the time, the question was puzzling as I had not yet received any payment for my writing. Only later, after immersing myself in the writing and submitting process, would I learn about professional rates. When I submitted my first science fiction story, I was simply overjoyed that it had been accepted for publication. Receiving the complimentary copies of the anthology and seeing my words in black ink was just milk in my garri—a delicious extra.

There is a certain freedom that comes from being compensated for your work with actual money, and not just the patronizing assurances of exposure. That feeling of validation hits differently. I should make clear that being unable to pay contributors because volunteers are doing the bulk of the work is understandable, as opposed to those who don't value the work creatives deliver. These latter sorts appear to hold a number of opinions: that the writer should be more concerned with changing the world one word at a time; and that with more time on their hands they could write just as easily—and with much less effort.

Exposure is to be coveted when one is starting out, but as a writer grows in skill and confidence and quality of work produced, she should be paid for her art. Recall the nagging plot points you agonize over, the deadlines that cause your belly to flop in an I-think-I'm-going-to-be-sick fashion, the insecurities that set up camp in your living room and demand water and snacks? Those ones? If you are able to knit sentences and paragraphs together into a doily that someone somewhere wants to decorate their space with—or as a sweater to be worn—then you deserve some payment for the wool.

Payments are sweet but irregular at best, and eventually the *ching-ching* of dollar signs in the starry writer's eyes will dull to the reality of the unpredictable writing life. It is a life fraught with waiting: for the words to come, for them to then blend into a cohesion you are bold enough to share, then for those words to be considered, and finally, for the rejections or the more elusive acceptances to come.

So, for me the lure of writing speculative fiction isn't the money. It is the boundlessness of worlds, of ideas, of imagination; no net below, no sky above. The accommodation the genre gives us all surpasses many a mother's arms. In it, I have found a community of writers that on certain levels feels like a functional family, one working towards similar goals and supporting each other along the way.

My stories stem from my joys and anxieties and griefs, the explainable and the not-so-much, and take unexpected twists and turns into magic, myth, or mystery. And, unlike most of the speculative stories I read growing up, I can infuse them with my traditions and folklore: boju-boju and Madam Koskos. Or they could be a hybrid of all those influences, my totality as a female Black African feminist wife mama.

From the day in the third grade when Miss Preston gifted me a white folder for writing the best creative work, I have been on this challenging, rewarding journey. In some respects, I have only just begun. I have gained experience as I plod on, floored but encouraged by the unstinting support and generosity of fellow travelers and comrades.

No matter the bad-mouthing and the bad reviews—or the non-reviews, those chunks of time where we feel invisible—we writers are fashioned from more resilient material. Ours will long outlast the barbed tongues, stalled expectations, and mere dislike. And that is the most liberating, beautiful thing.

Hannah Onoguwe's stories have been published in *Adanna, Imagine Africa 500*, and the *Strange Lands Short Stories* anthology by Flame Tree Press, as well as in *PerVisions, Litro, The Drum Lit Mag, Eleven Eleven, Omenana, Timeworn Lit Mag, The Missing Slate,* and *Mysterion Online,* among others.

She won the Association of Nigerian Authors Bayelsa Chapter poetry competition in 2016 and was shortlisted for the 2020 Afritondo Short Story Prize. She is currently a 2021 Climate Imagination Fellow at the Center for Science and the Imagination at Arizona State University.

She lives in Yenagoa with her family.

Writing Outside the Frame
A homeland called Palestine

Ibtisam Azem

You ask: What is the meaning of "homeland"?

They will say: The house, the mulberry tree, the chicken coop, the beehive, the smell of bread, and the first sky.

You ask: Can a ward of eight letters be big enough for all of these, yet too small for us?

— Mahmoud Darwish[1]

What becomes of Palestinians—or other colonized people—when they are not in the news, or when the camera is turned off? After the journalist is done writing their piece, what happens to the characters? Perhaps the artist, or the novelist, is the one who remains with them to tell their stories.

As a writer who was born and raised in Palestine, I am occupied by the question of how to write about a Palestinian reality that is complicated, both socially and politically. A reality that seemed, at times, to be stranger than what is imagined in fiction or films.

So, I try to write about the lives of Palestinians who are outside the frame. One of the ways I have chosen to do this is through magic realism and speculative fiction. This style has allowed me to hold a mirror to the cruelty and absurdity of an oppressive society and its policies, and to represent the inner worlds of my characters in a way that frees me from an often cumbersome reality.

---

1. Mahmoud Darwish, *In the Presence of Absence* (Brooklyn: Archipelago Books, 2011. Translated from the Arabic by Sinan Antoon).

I will discuss some of my works which employ this style. But before that, I wish to speak of the context of the lived reality of my characters and how that reality influenced me as a writer.

On the Homeland and the State. When I was seven, my maternal grandmother told me about their displacement, and I was astonished. My first reaction was: Why? My next question—one I often posed back then without realizing how painful it was— was: What happened? How come all of your family ended up as refugees outside Palestine, but you stayed here?

From 1947 to 1948, Zionist forces, which later became the Israeli army, displaced over 750,000 people. Terrified by the news of several massacres, such as at Deir Yassin and Tantura, more than half of the Palestinian population was forced to flee out of Palestine. After Zionist leaders declared the "independence" of Israel on seventy-eight percent of the land of Palestine, which was until then under British occupation, they didn't allow any of the displaced to return to their homes. Palestinians call this The Nakba,[2] The Catastrophe.

The small number of Palestinians who survived and stayed within the new state's border, about 150,000 people, became "citizens." Yet despite their status, they lived under military rule for the next 18 years, until 1966. In 1967, Israel occupied the rest of historic Palestine (the West Bank, East Jerusalem, and the Gaza Strip), as well as the Syrian Golan and the Egyptian Sinai Peninsula. It "gave" the latter back after a peace agreement with President Anwar Sadat's Egypt in 1979.

Many of those who were displaced by Israeli forces became refugees. They and their descendants, around five million people, are still not allowed back by Israel despite their "right of return," which was granted to them by international law and several UN resolutions. They are still living in camps in the countries they fled to—Jordan, Syria, Lebanon—and are still internally displaced in the West Bank and Gaza.

Israel did more than displace Palestinians in 1948. It also

---

2. See Ilan Pappe, *The Ethnic Cleansing of Palestine* (London: OneWorld, 2007).

destroyed 500 out of around 1,000 Palestinian villages, razing
them to the ground, and depopulated eleven Palestinian cities,
including Jerusalem, Jaffa, Lid, Ramla, Haifa, Akka, and Safad,
emptying them of their majority Palestinian inhabitants. All over
the country, whenever one sees a prickly pear cactus plant and
scattered stones, there you will find the remains of one of those
destroyed villages.

The majority of their land confiscated, any of the Palestinian
farmers who remained were forced to become laborers. Once-
flourishing cities and green villages were marginalized, and the
Palestinian neighborhoods and towns inside Israel became more
and more like ghettos.

Today, Palestinians live under different systems of settler
colonial rule, occupation, and apartheid. Israel applies different
rules and laws to each "group" of Palestinians who live under its
control. Each group—those within proper Israel (twenty percent
of the population, about two million people), those in the West
Bank and East Jerusalem (more than three million people), and
those in the Gaza Strip (more than two million people) has a
different legal status, but all of them are subject to racism and
discrimination at all levels. There are more than sixty-five Israeli
laws that discriminate against Palestinians inside Israel and the
territories it occupied in 1967.[3]

Escaping the "trap" of trauma when writing about Palestine.
From a very young age, I had to learn to navigate several parallel
worlds.

My father's family were farmers who were not displaced
from their town, Tayibe. But my mother's family were internally
displaced from Jaffa in 1948 and sought refuge there. I was born
and grew up in Tayibe, one of the ghettos where the Palestinian
citizens of Israel live, in the 1980s and 1990s. Yet I lived in a state
that didn't acknowledge my very existence as a Palestinian.

The curriculum in our Arab schools was Israeli. This meant
that we studied Hebrew literature. When we learned about

3. https://www.adalah.org/en/content/view/7771

modern Jewish history, it was mostly about European Jews. Arab and non-European Jews only made an appearance to bolster the official Ashkenazi Zionist narrative. Even when we studied Arabic literature, Palestinian literature was absent. I still recall that strange feeling of having to read Zionist literature at school that claimed that Palestine was "a land without a people for a people without a land." Before the spread of the internet, our only sources for our own stories were smuggled and pirated books and the oral history of our ancestors.

Overnight, in 1948, my grandparents became "citizens" of the new state of Israel, which—for them—seemed to have fallen from the sky. Everything around them changed: their symbols, their official language, even the landscape, which was changed to suit the "western" nature of the new state. Israelis planted trees, such as pines, that they had brought with them from Europe.[4] My grandparents were cut off from their relatives and from other Arab communities, becoming a minority in their own homeland. And they were not allowed to call that homeland by the only name they knew: Palestine. My grandparents and parents spoke of neighborhoods and towns that don't exist on the official map. Only cactus plants bear witness to them.

The prickly pear cactus, which originally came from the Americas, has become an important symbol of resistance and perseverance in modern Palestinian culture and collective memory. Its Arabic name in the Palestinian dialect is "sabir" (which also means "patience") and "sabbar" in written Arabic.[5] The plant was used by Palestinian peasants in their villages as a fence for their land, and it bears a sweet yellowish orange fruit. After the Nakba, many Palestinians saw its capacity to withstand drought as a parallel with their own resilience.

The cactus formed a fence for the edge of my parents' garden in Tayibe, where I was born and raised. My father still

---

4. This had negative effects on the environment, because these trees were more susceptible to fires in some areas. Other plants consumed too much water.
5. The word for the Palestinian cactus has been appropriated by Israelis to refer to Jews who were born in Palestine, called the "sabra" in Hebrew.

loves the plant and is fond of harvesting its sweet fruit. But from a young age I felt as if it was a trap, as well. Being born into this history, the more I grew, the more I felt that it was also growing within me.

One of the questions that occupies me as a writer is how to express my characters' choices and lived realities in a three-dimensional way, without becoming too documentary or journalistic. In my personal life, it was often "minor" events that left the biggest imprints in me. Those microaggressions went deep under my skin and still get triggered, even though I live thousands of miles away from Palestine, in New York City. Those injuries cannot be measured by listing the numbers of the wounded, displaced, or murdered.

Because in the middle of narrating the trauma and war, we often forget that life has its moments of joy, love, and laughter. That lived reality is not only the cactus's thorns; it is also its sweet fruits. And yet, how can you balance it? It is creativity, and in my case literature, that can do that.

While I don't frame my own writings in one restricted genre, one of many influences on me was the Russian philosopher Mikhail Bakhtin's ideas of the "carnivalization of literature." Magical realism, speculative fiction, the grotesque, and polyphony provide me with unlimited resources to critique a complicated lived reality, to turn matters upside down, to question reality and dig deeper into the lived experience of my characters. They also provide an unbreakable mirror to expose the emperor. They allow me the freedom to express and to innovate.

Writing speculative fiction and magical realism fiction about Palestine gives me the opportunity to see beyond the cactus's thick skin and thorns to the full plant with its sweet fruit inside.

Putting those who disappeared back on center stage. Although I had started experimenting with speculative fiction and magical realism in my first book, the chapters were relatively short and closer in their form to short stories. In my second novel, *The Book* *of Disappearance,*[6] the narrative revolves around the surprising and inexplicable disappearance of all Palestinians in historic Palestine, which turns reality on its head.

The novel focuses on the sociopolitical consequences of this fantastic event in Tel Aviv and Jaffa, due to the symbolism of these two cities in modern Palestinian and Israeli history. It is also occupied with what happens when a colonial society (Israel, in this case) whose national myth has been structured around the existence of an "enemy," suddenly loses that enemy. It mirrors the actual forced disappearance of most Palestinians from their land during the Nakba. But this disappearance, which in the novel takes place without a single drop of blood, becomes a character in and of itself.

This process gave me the space to present a complicated portrait of characters and how they react to an old/new reality. On one hand, it empowered the disappeared Palestinian characters, who are now disassociated from the fate of their rulers, and allowed them a respite of sorts. Through this sudden act of disappearance, they are, for the first time—as a collective and individually—free from the strictures that have been put in place to control them and their bodies and their narratives. They can now retreat quietly and tend to themselves, far away from their oppressors. On another level, this disappearance is a kind of warning of a future fate. A possibility of the repetition of another Nakba.

This "game" of narrating would not have been complete without the voice of the disappeared themselves. Alaa, one of the Palestinian characters, is able to speak through his journal which is found by his Israeli neighbor, who begins to read it. Alaa's descriptions of his fond memories of his grandmother, which no one wanted to hear before the disappearance, move to the center. Now everyone wants to listen to them because they are looking for "answers."

To make sure that the Palestinian narrator's voice doesn't get filtered through the neighbor who took over his apartment,

---

6. Ibtisam Azem, *The Book of Disappearance* (Syracuse University Press, 2019). Translated from the Arabic by Sinan Antoon.

the journal entries were written in separate standalone chapters. In this way, the marginalized characters remain at the center and cannot be displaced or exiled again.

When talking about Palestine and what happened during the Nakba and after, I often hear those who say that Palestinians are too occupied with the past, that they should look forward and just try to improve their lives. I was told to forget and move on. It is an argument often used to silence brown and black persons when they talk about historic injustice. But in fact, Palestinians, like other oppressed groups, do look forward and want to change their reality. For they want to make a better future and not repeat the past.

This is where speculative fiction, for me, can be useful. It is a type of literature that opens the door to possibilities without fear. The strange realities it presents provide a safe place for readers to engage with the worlds of the oppressed, worlds they would perhaps prefer not to go into. It can also become a weapon for me as a writer to not only to expose past injustices and their meaning, but to express our desire to change the future.

Writing as a way of finding home. I left Palestine when I was twenty-three years old.

I had reached a point where I felt that to stay would mean a slow death. If inside every Palestinian there is a homeland of cacti growing, the one inside me was losing its fruit. As a feminist Palestinian woman living in a settler colonial state, I had a bitter feeling that staying in a homeland where the prickly thorns of the cactus seemed to increase while its sweet fruit decreased would mean eventually not a fruit would remain.

When I left, it was only supposed to be for a few years. "Just to breathe," I said to myself. More than twenty years have passed, and it still feels like yesterday, though I return regularly to visit my family, and for research or work.

Although my fiction involves other worlds beyond those of Palestinians, I still mostly write about life under "the first sky." Fiction writing brings me home, but what speculative fiction and magical realism do for me is to enable me to use irony and laughter to process and work peacefully within that home.

In my next novel, a work in progress, I'm considering using, once again, a combination of magical realism and speculative fiction. I want to work with the subject of drugs and organized crime and their effects on Palestinian society in Jerusalem, Jaffa, and my hometown of Tayibe.

This is based on one of those childhood memories that is still crouching in a dark corner in my memory. I was lying on my back listening to the radio, staring at the ceiling of a room whose cracks had widened since last winter, when the sound of five or six gunshots pierced the chatter. I jumped to the window, which overlooked a snaking street lined with tiny shops on both sides that led to a mosque. People had left the shops and the mosque and were crowded around the corpse of a murdered man. The man was a major drug dealer, or that is what was said. The murderer went back to the car that he came out of and fled, just like that.

That was not the first or last murder in my hometown. Violence was, and is, still rampant in the cement thickets of these villages and towns. The only time Israeli police appeared in our cities and neighborhoods was when they determined that one of us constituted a "security threat" to the state.

Years later I became familiar with another death in a family who were our friends and whose son was killed by Israeli police because he was, allegedly, a big drug dealer. That time I didn't hear the gunshots, since they were fired in Jaffa, about forty kilometers south of Tayibe. But I saw the fear and heard the stories. Yet, the complicated story of that family goes back decades.

Although the novel will explore the connections between drugs and politics and land confiscations through a ghost story, it will also tackle social issues and challenges within Palestinian society. Here, too, I feel I can use speculative fiction and magical realism to touch on taboos in a way that doesn't drive the reader away, but rather involves them and compels them to engage. Or to put it in James Baldwin's words ...

"Societies never know it, but the war of an artist with his society is a lover's war, and he does, at his best, what lovers do, which is to reveal the beloved to himself and, with that revelation, to make freedom real."[7]

NEW YORK CITY
NOVEMBER, 2022

---

7. https://openspaceofdemocracy.files.wordpress.com/2017/01/baldwin-creative-process.pdf

Ibtisam Azem is a novelist, short story writer, and journalist. She works as a senior correspondent covering New York and the U.N for *Al-Araby Al-Jadeed* newspaper. She was co-editor and editor of the Arabic section at *Jadaliyya* e-zine. Prior to that she worked in Berlin as a journalist and editor for Deutsche Welle TV Arabic (DW-TV).

Azem holds an MA in Islamic Studies, with minors in German and English Literature from Freiburg University, Germany and an MA in Social Work from NYU.

She has published two novels in Arabic. Her second novel, *The Book of Disappearance (Sifr al-Ikhtifa)* was translated into English (Syracuse University Press, 2019) and Italian (Hopefulmonster, 2021) and is forthcoming in German (Lenos, in 2023). Her first short story collection is forthcoming in Summer of 2023.

In Defense of Circumstantial Villainy

Joel Donato Ching Jacob

I am the villain here, keep this in mind.

On the night of an informal high school reunion, five years after we graduated, my friends and I rented a small private pool resort to celebrate our first year in the workforce. Some of us were in postgrad, medicine, or law, but many of us were just excited to be on our own.

Way past midnight, and after a lot of drinks, my ex-girlfriend Kadison (not her real name) asked me if I ever loved her. I had come out as gay since we parted ways, and news would have of course reached her. I must have been on my seventh beer, but her question pulled me back to sobriety. I wanted to ease her fears. So, I said yes. That I loved her when we were dating.

It was a lie. I knew I was lying, but I lied anyway. My friends would tell me afterwards that having a "beard" was a bad thing, but there is a certain safety to be had when one can hide behind having a girlfriend whenever the world calls your swishiness gay. It didn't make it OK, but many gay guys do it. Kadison kept people from questioning if I was straight—including me.

Back then, I did not have a complete understanding of myself; I wouldn't have known that I wasn't straight. But it took me almost as long to figure out the truth. So, my villainous ways would not end there.

In a Catholic society like the Philippines, being straight was not just the default; it was the norm. Here, the Holy Family is enshrined as the standard. Telenovelas on TV show dashing men and graceful women falling in love despite the odds. Being gay is not just an outlier, it is considered abnormal. But even gayness had its rules. On Filipino media, gay men are depicted as being feminine. They are the lead woman's best friend and loyal to a fault—to martyr levels, even. Love is their singular driving force, though any romantic attraction they feel is used as comic relief.

As an effeminate man, what was I supposed to think except that I was gay? I was wrong.

Throughout college, I lied about not being a virgin. I was waiting to fall in love and was frustrated that it wasn't happening. I was twenty-four when I met Neph (not his real name) through blogging. LiveJournal, if internet archaeology is accurate. Neph was into geek stuff like reading, sitcoms, and space opera. I was into parties, food, and fashion. I don't know how our paths intersected, but they did, and Neph and I met up in real life. Neph loved me so much, it felt good. And I thought I loved him, but I loved him like—and as much as—a shiny new handbag. He looked good and I loved the way I looked with him dangling on my arm. I didn't feel more worshiped than when we made love. Well, Neph made love to me. I just had sex.

The concepts of Sexual Orientation and Gender Identity did not arrive in the Philippines until the last decade or so. Even then, they were met with resistance, at worst, and curiosity, at best. I did not question the label I had lived with for three decades. I was a gay man. Except, I was a terrible boyfriend.

Maybe I was quick to fall out of love? Maybe I hadn't met the right guy yet? I don't know. What I did know was that, as the list of men who hated me was getting longer, I was hungry for an ideal that books, TV, and movies made me believe I wanted. Or maybe I did want it out of a sense of normalcy, like a beard. But I never loved them. I did not need them. I just sought the safety of their affection. I led each one of them on because I was leading myself on.

Coming out as aromantic at forty years old means I have misled so many people over the decades. But there was no one

I misled more than myself. To each person I hurt, to Kadison, Neph, and all the many others after them, I am sorry. I am the villain. I am not making excuses, but I hope an explanation will do: I am aromantic—aro for short. I do not develop romantic feelings towards other people. Unlike people who primarily identify as asexual (or ace), I do feel sexual attraction and I often develop filial or familial love towards the people whom I am sexually intimate with, but never romantic love.

I believe that mainstream media is molding many young aromantic minds into villainy by enshrining romance as the end goal of interpersonal interactions between two individuals. What if—hear me out—all these toxic, emotionally unavailable trainwrecks are aromantic but have been gaslit to perform the rituals of romance at the expense of others? What if they are looking for romance because they were raised to expect as much? I do not want to be defending these jerks, but here I am.

I never had an aro role model growing up. Maybe if I did, I would have hurt fewer people along the way. That's why I want to write stories about aromantic experiences so that young people can see these stories and know that romantic love does not have to be the end-all and be-all for every person. That the fairy tale prince and princess can be friends without any excess baggage. That we can be driven by kindness and a sense of community, instead.

I wrote my novel Wing of the Locust with that in mind. The story is about an effeminate young man named Tuan who is recruited to become a kind of mystic called a mambabarang. The main plot aside, he attracts the attention of a childhood friend named Gilas, who offers him affection. Having been outcast all his life, Tuan has never been the recipient of kindness before. He is flattered but unsure what to feel, whether he can even trust another person. Nor can he trust his own feelings; the whole thing is alien to him. In the end, Tuan contemplates romance, rejects it, and faces the consequences from there.

I wrote the Wing of the Locust with the intent of featuring an aro character, but I have read reviews of it that range from shipping the two characters outright, to outright foreseeing a coupling between them in the future. Even a friend of mine who was a scholar of Filipino Queer Literary Theory, said that he was excited for the romance that would bud between the two characters. This was the opposite of my intention. I wanted to depict a connection between two men—one romantic, the other platonic—that resolves itself amicably.

This friend said that I "should throw Tuan a bone." Meaning, the kindest way I could write this character is to give him a romantic happy ending. He even says that it will bolster my sales. Who wouldn't want sales?

But I must stand my ground, I want to write an aromantic story despite how much more marketable it would be otherwise. I want to relieve young ace and aro people of the pressures of having romantic love and a relationship or partnership as an end goal. So there, spoilers! Tuan will be happy being single. Thank you.

Another friend questioned the need to even start a romance in *Wing of the Locust* only to write it into "failure." But it's not failure, it reflects how aro people experience a society that expects romance from them. Did I ever look at a romance with envy? Did I ever contemplate how much easier life would be if I could be romantic? Yes, and yes, but this is the same contemplation humans have made when looking at birds flying. A person can see the beauty and ease of flight without feeling that not having wings makes them incomplete.

I am complete without romance, but society is built so that I am made to crave it to fit in. Writing about the aro experience must include this unwilling immersion, as well as how the aro self unmires from it. I have to build up the possibility of romance; I have to make the characters contemplate it; only then can I write the rejection of the notion of romance without vilifying any of the characters. Are my stories anticlimactic because of this? Maybe. But then I am dealing with the same expectations that I lost myself to for decades.

A good story is a good story, they say, and the craftsmanship alone should suffice to appeal to the reader. But publishing is still heteronormative, even queer stories often fall into gender roles like their straight counterparts. Aromantic stories threaten their sense of normalcy. If I was myself convinced of the necessity of romance, how can I make my reader and prospective publisher believe otherwise? So, I am still striving to find markets for my stories that depict the disinterest for romance.

I am the villain here, and despite being more aware of myself, despite having the good intentions of creating more aromantic role models in fiction, I still am the villain.

Joel Donato Ching Jacob is author of the 2018 Scholastic Asian Book Award winner for *Wing of the Locust*, and its sequel, *Orphan Price*. He is also 2021 Clarion West Writers Workshop cohort. Cup, as he is called by friends and colleagues, is a full time HIV/AIDS volunteer counselor. He enjoys fitness and the outdoors. He lives in Bay, Laguna, with more dogs he can handle, plus a cat.

How Will You Use Your Voice?

Julia Rios

I'm bisexual, nonbinary, and half-Mexican, and I deal with chronic pain. These aspects of my identity have shaped who I am and how I perceive the world, and they've helped me realize that there are many other perspectives outside my own. When I am lucky enough to spend time in communities with others who share some of my specific identity markers, I always learn more about the struggles and triumphs others are having all around me.

Even if we frequent the same BIPOC and LGBTQ+ spaces, a Black trans woman will have a very different set of experiences than I do. If she takes the time and spends the energy to share her experiences with me, it's a gift, and I have learned that there is nothing so valuable I can do with my time as to listen. But even though I love expanding my perceptions of humanity, I've spent a lot of time as writer wondering how to tell my own stories—and which stories are mine to tell in the first place.

I have not been to Mexico since I was a teen, and my father has been dead for twenty years. Is anything I write "authentically Mexican"? No—I think—but also yes because I cannot disentangle myself from my experiences as a child of an immigrant. Any time I sit down to write, I ask myself why I am drawn to writing. What do I want to say, and, if I know that someone somewhere may be listening, how will I use my voice?

One reason we end up with so many persistent cultural stereotypes about marginalized people is because some people feel they have the right to tell others' stories in ways that end up causing harm to the real people living them. I feel strongly that I cannot and should not try to speak for Mexicans who are currently in Mexico or who have firsthand experience of immigration. People who wish to read about those experiences can look to authors like Gabriela Damián Miravete (whose short story about femicide in Mexico, "They Will Dream in the Garden," won the Otherwise Award a few years ago) and David Bowles (whose works like My Two Border Towns show a real glimpse into everyday life for Mexicans who live in border towns in and around southern Texas).

Sometimes I write stories where my Mexican heritage factors into the plot. Other times, I don't. Some of my stories feature characters who are queer; others don't. Even if a story does not overtly reference my ethnic heritage, gender, or sexual orientation, I care that it should stand as a sampling of something I value, one way or another. And what I value often boils down to empathy and community. Any story I write is a message to myself, first and foremost. Whether it's horror or comedy or wondrous fantasy, at the heart of it will be a question I cannot stop turning over in my mind, or a sentiment I want to see more people embrace.

These values apply to my editorial work as well. I know that with every project I agree to do, every time I send editing notes to an author, I am consciously using my curatorial power and editorial voice to help bring more of what I personally care about into the public sphere. This is true even (maybe even especially) when the project seems frivolous on the surface.

I believe that we all need a varied media diet. It's all well and good to have serious and substantive works that dig deep into the hard issues, but we also sometimes need to escape those hard issues. Traditionally marginalized people may need that even more often than others. If you are dealing with the constant onslaught of racism, ableism, sexism, homophobia, and other types of bigotry and discrimination, every little thing may feel harder for you than for a person who has the privilege of being able to ignore some or all of those things. Sometimes it's good to have a break, and I believe effective breaks can only happen when you feel safe and supported in the escapes you choose.

In the end of 2020, I decided to start a magazine called *Mermaids Monthly*. It had been a very difficult year. I was sick for a lot of it, beginning in March, when the world at large still didn't know much about how COVID was spreading, let alone how to treat it. Before I got sick, I was already on the edge of burnout, then I faced many rough months of recovery from what we now know as long COVID. On top of that, like most everyone else I knew, I was dealing with major social isolation. Outside my bubble, there were countless stories of police violence, the horrors of ICE detention, possible election fraud, and more. It is impossible to exist in the world as a person of color and not care about those things, but at the time I was mostly focusing on trying to breathe and keep my heart rate at a manageable level. Thinking about the news cycle, or my own work, was nearly impossible thanks to low energy and brain fog.

When I finally recovered enough to think about working again, all I wanted was a fun and whimsical project. So I chose something that seemed both aesthetically pleasing and like a big change from my previous projects: a magazine dedicated to mermaids.

I deliberately set some boundaries to keep my first big post-COVID project low stress, the firmest being that it would only last one year: twelve months of shiny mermaid stories. I partnered with Meg Frank, who is a truly brilliant art director, and we made a plan to raise money via Kickstarter and publish issue one of *Mermaids Monthly* in January of 2021.

You might think a magazine of mermaid stories would be pretty simplistic; certainly, one could fill a whole year with only Hans Christian Andersen retellings. But I wanted to go beyond those. To start with, we commissioned our first artwork and lead story from two Black creators. L.D. Lewis wrote us a story called "From Witch to Queen and God," and Nilah Magruder made an illustration for it that we used as our first cover. We also invited

Ashley Deng, a Canadian-born Chinese-Jamaican writer, and Lis Hulin Wheeler, who is autistic and of Lebanese descent, to join our team. Ashley came on board as assistant editor and Lis became our Logistics Wizard. From there, we were primed to attract all kinds of mermaid lore from different perspectives all over the world.

Yes, we did have some stories that engaged with Andersen and with Disney's interpretation of his story, but we also had selkies and Mami Wata and sirenas and a really cool 10,000-word novelette by a Native author about islanders facing an evil cruise ship. We had trans mers and gay mermen and disabled mermaids and Black mermaids, some of whom were good and some of whom were villainous. We had pieces about families, those celebrating strong relationships, and those processing how to survive toxic ones. We had very young and very old authors at all experience levels, and from many parts of the world. Ashley and Lis had input on which pieces we selected and also chose to edit a few stories themselves. It was a wonderful experience. Meanwhile, every story I chose was a message from me to myself first, and then to everyone else: "Look at this!" I was saying. "Look at how many different kinds of voices there are—and look how cool it is to see different perspectives!"

The public reception of the magazine was very positive. We got a lot of feedback in which people told us that they were surprised at how good and varied the contents were. Many people let us know that they would like it to keep going after 2021. However, I was still convinced that my run as editor and publisher should end after one year. This was a boundary I had set for myself to keep me from getting burnt out, and I wanted to keep to that.

I identify as nonbinary, but I appear more femme than masc and was socialized female; these things definitely affect how the world treats me. One thing I have learned from listening to many others in my shared communities is that if we don't look after ourselves as individuals, others will continue to demand more from us until we are run into the ground. I have seen this happen to too many wonderful people, and I think BIPOC, and particularly those who are not cis men, are especially susceptible. There's a narrative society likes to cling to that says women of color are strong, so they should be able to handle extra—perhaps even infinite—pressure, right? I think this often leads to people offering them less support.

Even though I was committed to protecting my limited energy, I also agreed that it would be great to let the magazine continue beyond its initial year. I talked with Meg about it and we decided that if we were going to keep it going, we had to make sure it would continue to showcase many voices, especially traditionally underrepresented voices, not just among its contributors, but also on the editing and publishing teams.

To that end, Meg and I put out a call for BIPOC people who might be interested in taking over *Mermaids Monthly*. We interviewed several candidates and ultimately chose a team of four—Noelle Singh, Miyuki Jane Pinckard, Vida Cruz, and J.D. Harlock—to hand the magazine off to.

Our plan was to help the new team run a Kickstarter to fund another year and then step away. But it turns out a global pandemic is a tricky thing to navigate. In the middle of the fundraising period, multiple members of both the new and old teams came down with COVID. We had to step back, reassess, and ultimately cancel our Kickstarter.

Some people look at this period and ask how it feels to have failed. I can only say that it did not feel like failure to me. I feel that choosing to prioritize the health and safety of the people involved was much more important than setting people up to deliver things they might not have energy to create, particularly on the tight schedule a monthly magazine demands. My feeling is that *Mermaids Monthly* was a success in 2021, and it may become a new and different kind of success in the future.

As I write this essay in May of 2022, the new team has worked together to select and edit a group of lovely pieces for the thirteenth issue of the magazine, which is nearing the proof stage, where contributors will do a final check for errors. I don't know if there will be more issues after that, or if the team will remain the same. What I do know is that having a thirteenth issue is, in itself, a triumph and a bonus.

As for me, I continue to slowly regain my energy. It is a nonlinear process that involves surges and setbacks, but I'm still here. I'm still writing and editing, though more slowly than I was able to in the past. There are still many things I don't know. There are still areas where I am learning and listening, and where I need to ask questions before I can understand and appreciate how I still need to grow. I am very fortunate to be part of a thriving community of writers and editors and readers who are willing to share their experiences and perspectives.

I hope that if I do one thing with my writing and editing career, it's to connect with people and amplify our collective voices in the service of empathy. It's the only way I can see to create a world I want to inhabit.

Julia Rios (they/them) is a queer, Latinx writer, editor, podcaster, and narrator whose fiction, nonfiction, and poetry have appeared in *Latin American Literature Today*, *Lightspeed*, and *Goblin Fruit*, among other places. Their editing work has won multiple awards including the Hugo Award, and they've narrated stories for Escape Pod, Podcastle, Pseudopod, and Cast of Wonders. To find out more, visit juliarios.com.

Minding the Gap
On Navigating Reality Through Speculative Fiction

L.D. Lewis

I was on the stairs going down to dinner on a Thursday night when I gapped.

That's what I call those pivotal moments where a well-managed mania turns into something else. Gapping is when my anxiety reaches such a fever pitch that I stop trusting muscle memory and begin to hyperfocus on the movements of my body.

When climbing, do I bear the transference of my weight on my toes just as they graze the edge of the next step, or do I push my toes towards the back of the step first? Will I destroy my gait entirely if my heel touches down? When did I learn how to use stairs? How am I certain that I am doing it properly? There are so many ways to go *down* stairs badly. What if my toes overshoot the edge by a millimeter, or I step on something disastrous that I can't see, or my balance is too far forward ...

My manias characterize themselves primarily as an onslaught of impossible questions issued in the voices of old acquaintances. They can be contemplated endlessly—and have been, at breakneck speeds—but never answered. My illness has been exacerbated by years of treating it, first as an issue of discipline and then as a thing to be solved and survived for slices of time, with alcohol or whatever numbing agent I could find in pill form.

My twenties were not great.

Not long after the incident on the stairs, I was hospitalized; I'd become a danger to myself. Eventually, for eight weeks and three days, I lived as a ward of institutions with varying understandings of bipolar disorder. The time I spent under their watchful eyes complicated my relationship with time itself.

Group therapies were designed to rid us of the loneliness of our illnesses ... In our leisure time, we talked of hopes and dreams, our embellishments of the worlds and environments from which we found ourselves separated for the time being. We were young parents, aspiring business owners, tortured artists, first-timers, fifth-timers—all funny, all skilled, all with different relationships to reality.

Me? I wanted to be a writer. Well, so did a bunch of us. Everyone had been through something and had a memoir in their minds somewhere. Something gritty, something real, something that explained to people who they were or who they'd intended to be in the moments they had failed hard enough to end up in a place like this.

There was little talk of fantasy, probably because that wasn't the point of the place. Make-believe was for children. Dabbling a bit too hard in it is what had landed some of us there in the first place. Turned out I needed it, though. Hyperfixation on the details of worldbuilding, which is inherent in fantasy, was something less injurious to my functioning in the real world. I could plug my own eccentricities into fictional characters in a way that made these characteristics useful or lauded, or at least more interesting than fraught.

The result was 350,000 words: a lush, sensory, science-fantasy saga about a genius of a girl in a seaside town who is frequently told (and rejected because) she has "too much going on," until she discovers her quirks are actually keys to the fate of a world with an uncertain future. It was a work essential to my healing. It was my way of communicating with my own world, in a less horrifying, more fantastical fashion, the beautiful things my complicated brain was capable of—even while I'd been mostly consumed with the darkness of it.

With this new main character, the terror intrinsic in my hyperfocus became endearing. She used it to solve puzzles or to memorize the creases in a lover's hand. Her quiet demeanor, once rooted in my own social insecurity, just meant she was more observant than most. We shared a love of frybread and the need to process problem-solving through busying our hands with something else. There was a grandeur to her pastoral environment, something settled but storied and overwhelming— like a still from a Ghibli movie. Most importantly, and perhaps aspirationally, her existence is essential. She is needed, not incidental. By the end, I'd come upon the first time in my adult life when I'd been healthy enough to finish anything.

A year or so later, I began looking into publishing professionally: the traditional route. I'd finally finished something coherent and beautiful, and there was no reason to squander it.

The first harsh lesson I learned was that no one wanted a 350,000-word novel, much less a debut from a nobody. The second was that next-to-nobody wanted a fantasy of any length from a Black person, unless they were writing for children or about a specific historical horror related to being a Black person. All of this before I even started querying.

The behemoth text was finally split into a trilogy. The first third became the first book I ever queried, and the book that landed me my agent. Every rejection amounted to a new alteration to the storytelling, the characterization, the plot structure, so that it could fit whatever it was assumed the market wanted at the time. My central character had "too much" going on internally. The level of detail in the world, which had sustained me during my darkest days, resulted in "glacial" pacing. The flavor of the day was plot, action, breakneck speed to hold the attention of the busiest reader.

I landed an agent 149 rejections later. After more changes, it failed to sell on submission. They'll always say it's a matter of timing, of market conditions, that so much of publishing is subjective and not to take it personally. But given the place within me where this work was derived, how could I not? I considered that maybe in all the revisions, I'd stripped the soul from it. Maybe my heart no longer came across in the version I'd presented. The exact nature of my failure had become yet another impossible question for my illness.

To be clear, the story was never published. Not yet, anyway. It does however, continue to serve me in ways I hadn't expected. Other stories—shorts, novelettes, a novella—were birthed from this novel's universe and published to some acclaim over the years, so it hasn't been a complete loss. I've also thrown my obsessive nature into studies about publishing. That may be as much about trying to get to the root of my own rejection as the existential problem-solving of systems—I'm certain my therapist has an opinion. Maybe most importantly, it has served as an anchor to my past. I have 350,000 words worth of testimony on what lies on the other side of a gap.

And so here is the crux of it: what we write has to satisfy us first. It's the only guarantee we have that we are not wasting our time. There is no promise of publication, no certainty that our beta readers will actually read the work as promised, no assurance that our friends will understand it—even though they are supportive of us. Sometimes the furthest we can take our work is to complete it.

But if it's a story we can revisit in our own quiet hours and have it provide us with peace or motivation, or act as a stepping stone to some other goal, it will always have been energy well spent.

L.D. Lewis is an editor, publisher, and Shirley Jackson Award-nominated writer of speculative fiction. She serves as a founding creator and Project Manager for the World Fantasy and Hugo Award-winning *FIYAH Literary Magazine*. She also serves as the founding Director of FIYAHCON, Researcher for the (also award-winning) *LeVar Burton Reads* podcast, and she pays the bills as the Director of Programs and Operations at Lambda Literary. She also authors a number of studies about the treatment and experiences of racially/ethnically marginalized authors in speculative literature. She is the author of *A Ruin of Shadows* (Dancing Star Press, 2018), and her published short fiction and poetry includes appearances in *FIYAH*, *PodCastle, Strange Horizons, Anathema: Spec from the Margins, Lightspeed*, and *Neon Hemlock*, among others. She lives in Georgia, on perpetual deadline, with her coffee habit, two cats, and an impressive LEGO build collection. Tweet her @ellethevillain.

The Wayward Gods of Tamil Nadu, or the Case for South Indian Surrealism

M. L. Krishnan

Space. It was 2010, the summer of listlessness. I had just returned to Chennai[1] on a sabbatical, and had two weeks to myself before I traveled further south into rural Tamil Nadu to begin my new position as a field communications specialist for a nonprofit organization. I was hurtling down an indeterminate funnel of time atop a carousel of dubious life decisions, and I believed that the next job, the next miracle, would turn everything around for the better. But I had nowhere else to go in the interim, so I ended up at my parents' house.

I spent my days in a fog-limned inertia, smudged within a blur of Tamil TV channels. There were dozens of channels devoted to films alone—some of them hyperfocusing on a single actor-politician's filmography. News stations screamed with an unrelenting breaking-news chyron that looped scenes of school buses speeding over ravines, the latest sex racket of a local godman, and designer sweatpants worn by C-list celebrities roving through airports at almost every minute of every hour of every day.

One afternoon, as lethargy settled around my shoulders in a wet drape of heat, an episode of *Solvathellam Unmai* (*Everything I Speak Is the Truth*) flashed on. A bizarre three-way cross between talk-therapy,

---

1. I use Chennai and Madras interchangeably, as they refer to the same city. I was born in Madras and it was renamed Chennai when I was a teen, so both those names hold significance for me.

loud interpersonal drama, and the soft-glow sophistication of an investigative report, it was hosted by a former screen siren who had reinvented herself to stay relevant.

On this day, the primary guests were a couple on the threshold of divorce. Outfitted in their finest coordinated silks—the zari of his veshti matching the plum-hued pallu of her sari—they were twinned in their misery, even if their objectives were antithetical to one another.

The woman wanted to leave her husband for a local demigod, a divinity who had followed her home after she had carelessly left offerings at his roadside shrine. The spirit was ardent, pooling around the contours of her sleeping form every night. About a month into their affair, an epiphany knifed into the woman's conscious. She could not stay married anymore. She sat on that stage, her lashes beaded with tears, reciting the question *what else can I do* in an endless litany. The studio light pulsed like a dying sun in the background.

No one exclaimed surprise at her claims. Not the host, and not the audience. Everyone seemed to commiserate with the woman. After a useless bleat of protest from the husband, the screen siren waved him aside, moving on to her next set of guests without fanfare.

In the years that followed, I kept coming back to that episode of *Solvathellam Unmai*, the woman, her demigod, and the spaces they breached through the real and the irreal. In choosing the incorporeal over the flesh-and-blood marrow of her husband, his physical heft, the woman reclaimed her agency. And with her, all of us—the studio audience, the viewers, and the talk show host—were hauled into a space that jostled with the mundanities of a fractured marriage, the otherworldly, and the ease with which we acknowledged this surreality.

As a writer of experimental speculative fiction, I have always strived towards dismantling and reconfiguring the binary of what Tamil feminist scholar C.S. Lakshmi—or Ambai as she is more widely known—calls "inner-outer divisions" against the bas-relief of the tangible. This is how I attempt to map my unmoored, postcolonial state as a queer woman raised in South India. As an immigrant alien now living and taking up space in the United States.

Memory. It was the summer of doors. I had just turned nine, and my family had relocated to Bombay from Madras. We lived in an apartment complex that surged into a sea of flats, cresting over a thicket of intertwined streets. Grocery stores, cafes, and other oddments were ensconced within our complex, a vividly adorned door being the only identifying differentiator between a private apartment or a secret nightclub.

Every afternoon, I would set out exploring with my friends for the doors that glinted with promises. A midnight-hued door illustrated with French éclairs for a bakery. A butter-yellow door for the kitty party club where aunties met often to swill scotch and play bridge. A mathematics cram school that removed its doors altogether and replaced them with macramé curtains through which harried students whirled in and out, ceaselessly.

One fateful day, I came across a plain gray door taped with a ruled-paper sign that read "Lending Library."

For two rupees, I could hide in the Lending Library for as long as I wanted. From the horizontal-paned window, orange sunlight fell in bars of dust on the book covers. Like me, the librarian was also from Madras. She was a retired school principal who was mostly spectral, emerging only to collect my fees and fading into the burrow of her apartment right afterwards. I was completely unsupervised, so I read everything within physical reach. I read about a decade's worth of *Detective Comics*, starting from the issue when Odd Man first appeared; every Nancy Drew and Sweet Valley High volume; and every *Parade* magazine from the 1980s. I devoured Guy de Maupassant's 1887 short horror story, *The Horla*, one afternoon and walked home in a shimmering haze of fear. Every shadow and every movement made me twitchy and afraid. The line "we are so weak, so powerless, so ignorant, so small—we who live on this particle of mud which revolves in liquid air" evoking a wellspring of terror in me for weeks.

Having razed through hillocks of English books, my attention finally moved to the Tamil weeklies organized in a dim corner. Within their pages, I beheld illustrated girls who looked like me for the first time. Fish-eyed heroines with pierced noses trooped through adventures in half-saris or skirts or shorts, their hair piled atop their heads in wavy braids and cockscomb flowers. Yet, their stories were tantalizingly out of my reach, as I was incapable of reading or writing my native language.

At the time, I—like many middle-class Indians—attended a school where the medium of instruction was English. My school was established by the British during the Madras Presidency, when the region was an administrative subdivision of Colonial India and had scarcely changed its curricula in a hundred years. It continued to uphold the colonial project of forcibly cleaving us from our tongues. We were not allowed to converse in our native languages, the long shadow of corporal punishment ever present, looming.

That summer, a comic serialized in one of these Tamil weeklies stood out from all the rest. Its protagonist was a teenager in a school uniform much like mine—navy pleated skirt, buckled Mary Janes, red ribbons woven through her plaits. She would periodically metamorphose into a snarling, ravenous bear deity, only returning to her human form in the presence of what seemed to be her classmate or her boyfriend. I wanted to know more beyond puzzling together a mosaic of assumptions based solely on what I saw.

Building up my courage, I approached my grandmother with the magazine in the hopes that she would read it to me.

She simply said, *read it yourself.*

That marked the beginning of my Tamil lessons with Ammama. Under her caring yet firm tutelage, I regained my language, letter by letter. I learned to practice its curves first, and then through rote repetition, conjugate its grammar. The hazy bridge in my mind between the cadences of a spoken tongue and its intricate poetic and literary counterparts emerged into view.

As my lessons progressed, I began to haltingly read sentences in Tamil for the first time, then entire paragraphs, stories. I consumed all the other lurid weeklies from cover to cover. They drew me into a maelstrom of astonishing tales involving love, reincarnations, baroque murder mysteries, haunted wells, spirits that moved through humans and farm animals and gods with gusto—all set in my home state of Tamil Nadu. And finally, I could now read the story about the ursine high school teenager. About her thrilling adventures, her classmates, and the boy who loved all of her—the girl and the howling bear goddess, her teeth, the entrails she left behind.

Scar. It was the summer of hospitals. I was 27 years old and recuperating in the aftermath of a car crash. As my face was being stitched back together in crisscrossing lines across my eyelid and my forehead, the shape of my immediate future coalesced around a revolving door of surgeries and doctors' offices.

It was also election season in Tamil Nadu. This meant one of two things: The current actor-politician's party would continue to tighten its vise grip on power or it or would be usurped by a rival party helmed by another actor-politician. There were no other options, since Tamil cinema did not just encompass movies and their cultural import; they were divine vessels, springboards that could launch stars *and* initiate their political careers.

Tamil actors were deities, hallowed beings who wielded official titles such as Universal Hero, Revolutionary Leader, Acting Commander, and Emperor of Love. These titles were bestowed upon them by their fan clubs in ceremonies rife with pomp and adoration. Once, a schoolteacher pledged her tongue—the throbbing, muscular organ in her mouth—to the chief deity of Revolutionary Leader's childhood village, promising on TV that she would rip it out with a machete if her candidate lost. Another time, a taekwondo guru crucified himself for his preferred candidate, videotaping the entire process in arduous detail.

This was the way of Tamil Nadu politics.

Caught in that liminal teaspoon of time between harm and recovery, I was incapable of absorbing anything linear. Days and hours turned gossamer, fading out of reach. Books were elusive. I could not find the words to parse my broken body or the disjunctive political climate mounting to a fever pitch in my state.

I then read *Zero Degree* by Charu Nivedita.

A transgressive, postmodern novel set mostly in Chennai, it unspooled in a kaleidoscope of diagrams, punctuation-less chapters, epigraphs from the Bhagavad Gita, political mythmaking, questionnaires, receipts, and catalogs of all kinds. *Zero Degree* was slippery, profane, and indelibly Tamil. In its pages I had found a warped looking-glass, an arc of convergence for what I was experiencing while occupying several fractured states at once.

> *Which place are you from.*
>
> *Place means edam, space also means edam, face means mokam, race means ottam, case means case.*
>
> *Well means kenaru, wall means suvaru, wool means kambli, pull means izhu, full means fullu.*

Like the quoted sentences above, passages from *Zero Degree* frequently collapsed into dreamlike, enumerative lists or poetry. But in other instances, looping stanzas were interspersed with lines of exquisite tenderness: *Genny, go and touch the stretch marks on Aarthi's stomach. I want to kiss your fingertips while they linger there, caressing the roots of time.* I tried to wrap myself in the comforting quilt of cynicism, pull it up to my chin and lie in its folds, but sections such as these served as beacons, leading me towards something tangible, an existence finally taking form.

André Breton states in *The Surrealist Manifesto* that surrealism "asserts our complete nonconformism clearly enough so that there can be no question of translating it, at the trial of the real world, as evidence for the defense." As my flesh healed, I watched a news segment about the martial artist who had outlived his self-inflicted crucifixion from my hospital bed. While he answered the interviewer's questions from his own hospital bed, I realized that the martial artist and I were funhouse-mirror reflections of each other in that instance through our shared brokenness, our bed-ridden states. This is how I found myself adrift within one of

Breton's untranslatable moments, within the fluid theatricality of the everyday and the supernatural.

In furrows of imperialist trauma, we dwell amid a pastiche of haunted identities—both inherited and otherwise. As a part of the South Indian postcolonial experience, we hold languages and morals that are not our own, that were forced upon us via a spiritual and cultural scaffolding that is ours alone. This is why I write about unruly, non-normative bodies in the Subcontinent—like mine—through stories centered on the embodiment of identities coded as queer or feminine in the form of visceral physical transformations, especially of the ones we cannot control. I return again and again to characters who find themselves in the hazy borderlands between the tangible and the otherworldly. Between obsession and ritual. And in my work and my lived lives as a Tamil author of speculative fiction, I continue to explore this surreality, this perfectly natural state of being that eludes Western categorization, and complicates it.

M. L. Krishnan originally hails from the coastal shores of Tamil Nadu, India. Her work has appeared, or is forthcoming, in *Diabolical Plots, PodCastle, The Offing, Sonora Review, Baffling Magazine, The Best Microfiction 2022 Anthology, Death in the Mouth: Original Horror by People of Color*, and elsewhere.

Her stories have been nominated and shortlisted for Best of the Net, the *Best Microfiction* anthology, the Stabby Awards, the Bath Flash Fiction Award, the Coppice Prize, and more. She is a 2019 graduate of the Clarion West Writers Workshop, a 2022 recipient of the Millay Arts Fellowship, and a 2022–2023 MacDowell Fellow. Her chapbook, *The End, as Seen from the Tip of the Indian Peninsula* is the winner of the OutWrite 2022 Chapbook Competition (fiction), and is forthcoming from Neon Hemlock Press.

Enjoying / Employing the Margins

Malka Older

I particularly enjoy the experience of being in a new place where I don't speak the language or understand the customs of daily life. I love the newness of it: almost constantly seeing, smelling, or hearing something strange, stimulating, and fascinating to me.

I also like the learning curve. Starting from nothing means being empty and ready to absorb. I love hearing a set of sounds over and over again, picking out patterns and repetitions. I love the puzzle of piecing together the meaning of the word from the contexts. It's not just language, either: I love finding clues to the differences, the behaviors I don't understand—like slowly realizing, over a period of months, that there's a reason a lot of people wear yellow on a certain day of the week.

It's a learning both intuitive and active, where my brain works hard at listening and looking, but also finds connections while it's resting. When I moved to Japan, I struggled to remember the different strokes of the characters when I wasn't looking at them; then one night, lying in bed, I discovered I could trace with my mind's eye the prefectural kanji from the license plates I'd stared at while stuck in traffic.

There's also something about having a reason to be visibly and audibly an outsider. I never really felt like I belonged where I grew up. I was born there, but my parents weren't. I didn't look exactly right, I didn't talk exactly right, I celebrated different holidays. Since my parents were each born in different places, I didn't quite fit into either of their respective diasporas either, not fluent enough in the language, not quite getting all the jokes.

It was okay. I fit in within the confines of my small immediate family. And probably everyone feels like an outsider to some extent as they grow up. What I feel grateful for, now, is that I felt different enough not to bother trying too hard to fit in.

And so, when I left the place where I grew up for other cities and countries, I found a kind of comfort in officially, obviously, not belonging. Not belonging gives me permission to not understand everything. I get to try foods for the first time and decide whether I like them or not; I get to try new styles of talking, new personas even. I'm not required to hold predetermined opinions, because I'm an outsider, already assumed to be different, and when I'm excluded—when my religion or language or preferred gender expression or any other aspect of my identity is not considered—it doesn't hurt as much, because I never thought I would belong.

Besides the comfort of not feeling like I'm supposed to belong when I don't, it also highlights the learning curve I mentioned earlier. It's so much easier to learn when no one expects you to understand, when you can give yourself permission to be childlike and ask questions about things that are obvious to everyone else around you. This kind of blank-slate learning can be terrifying, and frustrating, but it's also intense, drenched in desperate observation and sudden, hard-learned connections.

This is the experience I think about when I'm introducing people to a new world in a book. I want the reader to be somewhat disoriented at first, because they are in a new place. The character they're identifying with might know what's going on, but the reader should feel alert and interested, fascinated and learning fast. I want their brains to be working, actively engaged in figuring out the subtexts of the world they've landed in. Fire up that imagination!

Whether it's running in the background or making a conscious effort to suss out the underpinnings of the world-building, as far as I'm concerned, that only adds to the verisimilitude of the reading experience. When I'm reading, I don't want everything handed to me; I'd rather feel that *ping!* of understanding when I figure something out, either after thinking through it or before even realizing that it was a mystery. There's a satisfaction that comes from having multiple levels of my brain working at once: the words I read, the images they conjure, the senses behind them, the gaps, and their fillings.

No matter how tropey it is, how central to a certain cultural milieu, how familiar it may be to some of us, as writers, we have to remember that the world we're writing is always going to be unknown to some of our readers. This goes for any kind of story, whether it's speculative or not, set in the far future or through a fantasy portal, or in historical Kansas or Los Angeles, or present-day Tokyo or day-after-tomorrow rural Australia. There will be people out there for whom the setting is going to be entirely new—even if it is Brooklyn, New York, an anonymous suburbia, a British country house, or post-War Paris. We are *always* worldbuilding.

Even if the general setting is familiar, the world of the story should be as particular, as idiosyncratic and fully realized, as the characters. For those of us readers who know a place, who live in it, perhaps, isn't it better when the writer constructs it anew for us? If they immerse us in it, we will see something different; a shift in perspective that shows us that the massive tree we see from the second-story window looks smaller from the fourth floor. That triangulation, triggering both familiarity (or perhaps nostalgia) and newness, presence and absence, can add nuance and depth to our imagined setting.

Not everyone gets the same enjoyment from having no clue of what's going on as I do; not every reader is going to enjoy that part of my novels. That's fine. Not every book is for everyone. It's possible that a childhood of feeling like I didn't belong prepared me for not belonging in other places. I was primed to search for meaning in incomprehensible societal behavior, to adapt myself to not knowing. It was a painful skill to learn, but these days I'm okay with being the outsider. I feel comfortable—at least relatively comfortable—with being unsure. I enjoy the gush of the unknown, even the parts where I'm gasping in confusion.

That may seem strange; we should want everyone to like our work, right? There is a certain cherished ideal of universality that gets mentioned a lot: the idea that to be *art*, a book has to speak to everyone, has to communicate some aspect of life that is fundamental and unchanging. But that doesn't exist, as those of us on the outside know very well. It is a fetishization of the experience of insiders, of the people who belong, as being something that everyone can relate to equally. It's not. And being expected to relate makes me feel just as inexplicably wrong as I did as a kid growing up different.

As a reader, I'd rather have specificity than universality. Sure, it's great when a book clangs that deep harmony of recognition across difference, but for that to happen, it first has to be different. I don't want to read books about people just like me any more than I want to read books telling the same stories I've read in countless other books before. I want books that teach me what it's like to be someone else.

So, I don't mind if some people find my books too disorienting or difficult. I'm confident that enough people grew up as outsiders to enjoy my writing. Maybe there are more people who have had the experience of being *other* than there are people who feel like part of a universality.

I, at least, feel a responsibility to give all my readers some degree of confusion, a hint of that feeling of being in unknown currents and the seafloor dropping away from beneath their feet. I want to offer the struggle, the disorientation. Without that, the gradual, growing understanding doesn't mean as much.

And while I treasure that feeling of hard-won familiarity that makes it so hard to leave a book when it's over, I believe in the turmoil for its own sake, too. I want my readers to always know they're somewhere they don't entirely belong.

Some might see this as vengeance for growing up an outsider, but from me it is a gift.

Malka Older is a writer, aid worker, and sociologist. Her science-fiction political thriller *Infomocracy* was named one of the best books of 2016 by Kirkus, Book Riot, and the Washington Post. She created the serial *Ninth Step Station* on Realm, and her acclaimed short story collection *And Other Disasters* came out in November 2019. Her novella *The Mimicking of Known Successes*, a murder mystery set on a gas giant planet, will be published in early 2023. She is a Faculty Associate at Arizona State University, where she teaches on humanitarian aid and predictive fictions, and hosts the Science Fiction Sparkle Salon. Her opinions can be found in *The New York Times*, *The Nation*, *Foreign Policy*, and NBC THINK, among other places.

How I Shattered My Horizons

Millie Ho

I shuffled onto the glass bridge at Longgang National Geological Park and glanced down. Nothing but jagged rocks and a deep blue river in the valley below. If I didn't have a fear of heights before, I definitely had one now. The bridge was shaped like a horseshoe and jutted from a cliff. The green mountains and wispy clouds made me feel like I'd stumbled into a scene from some wuxia movie. I breathed in the frosty air and felt intensely alive.

"Do you have anything like this in Canada?" asked my cousin, a young man in a puffy yellow jacket. Behind him, my other cousins and their friends leaned against the glass wall and posed for photos, their cheeks rosy from the early-February chill.

"The CN Tower?" That was the last glass floor I'd walked across, an experience that now felt small in comparison to the vibrancy of our surroundings.

We followed the crowd of sightseers back to the main park area. There, we boarded a bus that would take us into the mountains themselves.

It was 2017, and I was in Chongqing.

I moved to Asia in 2016. An opportunity to travel presented itself, and I took it. My reasons were simple: I wanted to see more of the world, learn more about my heritage, and bring more stories to life.

I'd learned a long time ago about the benefits of exposing myself to something new. I grew up in North York, a part of Toronto with a lot of first-generation Chinese Canadians. My early years were spent watching Korean dramas, drawing manga, and debating which J-rock bands had the hottest members. My friends and I shared YouTube skits about strict parents and shouted catchphrases from then up-and-coming comedian Russell Peters's stand up show—"Be a man! Do the right thing!"—that proved people like us were visible enough to joke about.

But all the stories I wrote during that time featured white, male protagonists. I lived among Chinese Canadians in my community, spoke Mandarin at home, and consumed media by East Asian creators. So why did I hesitate to write stories about people like me?

Looking back, the answer was obvious: because all my favorite novels were written by and about white folks. My reading choices were mostly curated by my school library, which carried titles like J.R.R. Tolkien's *The Lord of the Rings* trilogy, Philip Pullman's *His Dark Materials*, and many Stephen King paperbacks. I'd internalized the belief that genre fiction had to look a certain way—and I wasn't it.

Fast forward a few years. I went to university and met other students who introduced me to authors like Catherynne M. Valente and Octavia E. Butler and to subgenres like cyberpunk and urban fantasy. I took courses that expanded my reading preferences and found a lot to like about other genres: the metaphors and similes of hardboiled detective fiction; the precision with which realist writers described contemporary North American life; the joy and brutality that oozed from the vignettes of Beat Generation poets.

Then I discovered magazines like *Lightspeed*, *Uncanny*, and *Strange Horizons*. In them, I found a treasure trove of diverse new voices. Writers crafted stories about strong female friendships, secondary worlds that weren't based exclusively on Europe, and superpowered queer protagonists. They coined terms like "silkpunk" and retold traditional myths in ways that reclaimed their own identities.

Bit by bit, I saw more people like myself on the page. Seeing others craft powerful, entertaining stories made me think that I could, too. Maybe I could also contribute to the diversity of the voices being published today.

The next question: How?

⟡

Just like how I needed to read beyond my school library to discover more authors, I needed to break out of my Canadian microcosm to deepen my understanding of the world and of myself. Only by removing myself from my existing environment could I shatter my horizons and grow as a person and writer/artist.

This was why I visited my hometown of Chongqing, a municipality in southwest China known for its mountains, spicy hotpot, and fast-growing urban areas. In Chongqing, I was no longer a minority—at least not in appearance. I raised eyebrows when I asked bus drivers to help me read directions in Chinese, but most of the time, I was readily accepted as part of the environment, a member of a larger identity. This removed a lot of the pressures of being in a new country and allowed me to focus on other parts of my trip.

Like social dynamics. I suddenly had aunts, uncles, cousins, and a bunch of extended family members I hadn't known existed. I felt like a child again, relearning how to function in society and in rooms crowded with people and food (most gatherings were in restaurants or someone's kitchen). The eldest member of your generation took care of the guest, so I stayed in my eldest cousin's apartment and shadowed her at work, where there was joking and warmth but also a very clear hierarchy. I accompanied my cousins' children to their stressful gaokao (standardized college entrance exam) review sessions, then watched them doodle heads, torsos, and legs in their school notebooks during rounds of exquisite corpse, a collaborative drawing game. I went to dinners where the seating order *really* mattered and braided the hair of a cousin's eight-year-old daughter when her mother didn't have time to do it before she left for work in the early morning.

I also learned about leisure activities. On weekends, I watched family members guzzle tea and shout at each other during heated mahjong games. At night, my cousins and I went to KTVs where we ate watermelon slices, played drinking games, and sang a lot of Backstreet Boys (the only English-language artist they knew) and Jay Chou (the only Mandarin-language artist I knew). I burned hell money to honor family members who had died before I was born and hiked up mountains in search of medicinal herbs, trailing after my cousin and his ten-year-old daughter as they traded facts about the plants they'd found. On a family trip to a temple along the Yangtze River, everyone joked that the mosquitos devoured me because they loved the taste of "foreign blood."

I rode the high-speed train into Chongqing proper, where skyscrapers pierced the hazy blue sky, no one used paper money (everything was paid by scanning QR codes), and Porsches zoomed down the same streets where people slept under cardboard boxes. I dropped in on trade shows and museums and learned about the massive socioeconomic advancements that had swept through the country in the last decade alone—but also about environmental destruction and the widening gap between the rich and poor. I went to a gym in the heart of the megacity where personal trainers hung around my treadmill and encouraged me to sign up for private training to get rid of my "problem areas," and I window-shopped in huge malls where boyfriends, weighed down by designer purses, shopping bags, and the occasional Starbucks order, followed dutifully after their partners.

I got to meet my grandmother before she died. She spoke to me in Sichuanese, and though I didn't understand, I nodded just to keep her smiling.

⌘

The more I learned about and experienced traditional and contemporary Chinese life, the more I was transformed, creatively and personally.

Myths and legends that were sparsely recorded in English or had been lost in translation were common knowledge here. Through my younger relatives, I received a crash course on the TV shows, video games, and serialized web novels that featured Chinese fantasy tropes, deities, and ancient kingdoms. On my last trip in 2019, the kehuan—science fiction—movie *The Wandering Earth*, adapted from Liu Cixin's story of the same name, was released and subsequently broke Chinese box office records. Relatives who were normally not into kehuan raved about it and encouraged me to read more translations of Chinese science fiction.

It became impossible not to see myself and those around me as the protagonists in these stories. The old belief that I didn't belong in science fiction, fantasy, and horror dried out and peeled away.

My years abroad not only normalized the idea that I could write about my experiences, but also provided the distance I needed to process them. Some ideas got condensed into poems that appeared in *Uncanny* and *Strange Horizons*. Other short stories were published in *Fireside*, *Lightspeed*, and *Nightmare*. A few, currently unpublished, led to my participation in the Clarion West Writers Workshop in 2019 and gave me other opportunities to learn and improve.

I was finally writing the kind of stories I would've loved to read when I was a kid. I was contributing to the magazines I'd admired all those years ago. And it was a thrill when I read someone else's story—set in an unfamiliar place, time, or universe—and found myself nodding at how relatable everything was.

We all have a front-row seat to the human experience. Traveling taught me that. If we ever think or feel something, chances are good that someone else has thought or felt them, too. In China, the details of people's lives were different, but the motivations and reasons behind their actions were the same. In the specific context of our lives lie the foundations of universally relatable stories.

At the Longgang National Geological Park in 2017, the bus dropped us off near the mouth of the cave. Neon-lit karst structures jutted above and below us like giant icicles. I followed my cousins deeper inside. It was colder than I expected. Our breaths came out in little white puffs. I tucked my hands into my pockets and tried to keep my teeth from chattering.

We stopped at the tallest structure—a knobby tower that stretched toward the ceiling—and lined up for photos. As I smiled at someone's camera, I thought of how the sharp mineral formations above their shoulder, cloaked in red, purple, and yellow light, looked like dragon teeth. And wouldn't it be interesting if the rainbow lights themselves weren't lights at all?

"Did you not sleep enough?" a cousin's friend asked me as we headed out of the cave. "You looked like you zoned out back there."

I shook my head. It was hard to explain.

She shrugged and took out a couple of milk-flavored candies from her purse. She handed me one and we ate the edible wrappers.

I followed her back to our group, colder and with a new idea about shapeshifting dragons in an alternate China—a novel I am writing today.

Millie Ho is a writer and artist based in Canada. Her short stories and poems have appeared or are forthcoming in *The Book of Witches*, *Lightspeed*, *Nightmare*, *Uncanny*, and elsewhere. Her work was a finalist for the Ignyte and Rhysling Awards. Find her at millieho.net.

What Should Not Be Broken

Nelly Geraldine García-Rosas

Imagine you are given a pottery bowl. A gorgeous piece of artisanship made by countless hands over many years in a faraway land. You worked hard to get it, maybe you even had to leave all your other earthenware behind. You are excited to use it, to display it in your new home for others to see, because it is yours now, and it is beautiful. But as soon as you touch it, you notice it is broken. You can see the cracks when you hold it, when you try to fill it and eat from it. You take it to the artisans and ask what is wrong with it. Nothing. There is no sign of damage while in its makers' hands. It is only broken for you, and because of you. You are told to accept that fact and go home with a broken bowl.

Imagine that bowl is the language you use every day. It is different from the one you grew up speaking, a language that you learned when you were a teenager. Suppose that the food you wish to serve in it is literature.

I was born and raised in Mexico. Being a middle-class girl there in the nineties and early two-thousands meant that most of the media and entertainment I consumed—movies and TV series, music, video games, even the magical and super slow internet—was created originally in English.

In my native country, learning and studying English is not

something that is usually done out of pleasure, but necessity. It is a very useful skill that could mean having better opportunities in every aspect of life. English literacy, though, creates a huge gap of inequality because it is still inaccessible to the majority of the population, particularly marginalized communities like indigenous and working-class people.

Despite our proximity to the US (and all the fuss created by the signing of NAFTA when I was a little girl), English lessons were not included in my elementary education curriculum. Middle school offered those classes, but, being a Mexican public school, they came with the caveat that the syllabus was flawed and some teachers were not properly trained. I had the privilege of attending a private high school with better lessons and a lot more pressure attached to them, even though I was placed in a beginner's level group. Later, one of my best friends, who had a degree in English, became my private tutor. He was the one who encouraged me to practice my newly acquired language by doing something I loved: reading speculative fiction.

The first book I read in English without a dictionary or a translator as intermediary was *A Wizard of Earthsea* by Ursula K. Le Guin, when I was in my early twenties. I had been taking English lessons for some years by this time, but I was still anxious about crossing the threshold into the stylistic devices and nuances of literary speech. To me, a person who was then pursuing a degree in Spanish and Latin-American Literature and to whom language was not only a form of communication but of art and living, it was distressing to confront a text like a novice. I felt so vulnerable, overtaken by my own ignorance. Words were my cornerstone, but in a foreign language they were indomitable and strange. I had already read *Earthsea* in translation, so it was a very peculiar and transformative experience approaching a story that was familiar and yet new to me. Each chapter felt like déjà vu, of wandering into a place where language created the world, where knowing the true name of things gives people power over them, where wizards have to learn a second language in order to work magic— like I do now with English and fiction.

I cannot recall the first time I heard the term "broken English." Although I do remember that during a trip to Yucatán I saw a sign hanging from a store window that read "Broken English spoken perfectly." It was placed as a joke to entice tourists to go in and buy souvenirs. A way to say it was a welcoming place for English speakers, to show that someone was trying their best to communicate and cater to the needs of others—even if those others thought their language had been broken in the process.

But a joke, even if it comes from a place of good intentions, can be painful.

When I became an immigrant, I understood that the way people like me write or speak in English is what others call "broken." Words coming out slowly due to self-consciousness, involuntary hyperbatons, a mind tired of being parsed looking for the perfect word again and again, grammar fumbled, mumbling because who knows what the correct pronunciation of that word or phrase only seen before in writing might be. Sometimes hating my accent, always being afraid of making mistakes.

And out of fear can come silence.

To break something is a violent act, a disruption. Even though others may think there is only one correct way to speak a living, evolving language, I do not want to believe that my trying to communicate or make art through fiction is a way of destruction. I do not wish to speak broken English perfectly, like that sign in Yucatán said, because I did not destroy anything. Nor do I want to be silent. I want to create. To bring myself, my past and my own speech into the language of my new home. I want to mend what should not be broken. Just like kintsugi[1] is used

---

1. "Kintsugi is the Japanese art of repairing broken pottery by mending the areas of breakage with lacquer dusted or mixed with powdered gold, silver, or platinum ... As a philosophy, it treats breakage and repair as part of the history of an object, rather than something to disguise." (https://en.wikipedia.org/wiki/Kintsugi)

to repair pottery and ceramics, I want to bring beauty into the apparent imperfections of my own personal way of speaking.

Thus, I speak and write in mended English.

◦✿◦

Imagine that you are hungry. You have not eaten in days because you had to go back home with a broken bowl. You are heartsore too. You do not know what hurts more, the hunger or the sadness. You sit alone because you cannot share the table with the artisans. And wonder if it would be easier to walk away and look for your old dishes, go back home and forget about the bowl. Or would it be easier to simply starve?

When thinking about your past, you remember the tiny pot of lacquer sitting on a shelf—the only thing you brought with you from your old home. It could be used to repair your bowl though it will not end up looking as pristine as it looks when the artisans hold it because this lacquer is of a different texture and color. But you are hungry. And you are sad. So, you roll up your sleeves and use the lacquer of your native land to mend every single crack of your new bowl.

As soon as the lacquer sets, you realize that your bowl is even more beautiful than before. It was made by countless hands in this strange land, but it was mended by you and you only with the soil you brought from your homeland.

Your heart flutters as you approach the artisans' table.

◦✿◦

One of the reasons why I write speculative fiction is because it is an amazing medium to explore otherness through words.

Since I left Mexico in my early thirties, almost eight years ago, I have become part of "the other," that immeasurable group whose commonality is of not belonging. I felt as if I was abruptly uprooted and left to dry. I was somehow not from there anymore, but not yet from here. And I felt lonely. It was through stories that

I was able to share and understand my own otherness, the liminal space that is myself.

Speculative fiction gave me a community that gets that I am a sorceress when I mix my prepositions, a time traveler when I get my verb tenses wrong, a monster breeder when I end up with unexpected phrases. Through my new language and my new home, I found that both this *me* and my stories do belong.

With the help and encouragement of editors and instructors, I got the validation and certainties I did not know I needed. Having the fortune of working with folks who are genuinely interested in my writing has been liberating. Unlike some Mexican authors and professors who tried to tell me that I should not write in my native language using calques or doing this or that, my English-speaking editors have asked me questions and made suggestions that have not been prescriptive because they do not want to change my fiction to fit a certain mold; they have been guides and not gatekeepers of proper, perfect language. At least the folks who have overseen my fiction do not seem to think I broke their language.

Some readers have been different, though. People on the street have been different. The editor who did not buy my story but sent a personal rejection filled with vitriol. The person who saw me with hatred when they heard me speaking with an accent. Maybe to them I am wielding a hammer I brought with me all the way from the city of my birth just to smash it against their language. And yet I keep on writing and speaking to show them that hammers can also be used with chisels to create new things.

There are many reasons why I write in English as a non-native speaker. It has become the lingua franca for genre fiction, giving it a huge readership. It is spoken in the places I have emigrated to (first the UK and now the US).

I cannot ignore that English is an imperialist language that has been imposed on many people throughout history. It is important to me to say that I am appropriating it, making it mine, mending it. My fiction exists thanks to it and in spite of it. In the end, it is a choice I made: a political, stylistic, privileged, personal one.

Gladly, I keep on having the kind of wonderful experiences that only a non-native speaker can have while experimenting with their other language: the exhilaration of discovery, frank wordplays and new idioms with never-italicized phrases, the freedom and innocence to approach something for the first time but with a trained eye. In the boundaries of my two languages is where I have found freedom.

Sometimes I feel like my journey as an exophonic[2] writer is not a straight line but a complicated road with curves and turns. Though I am confident that my stories matter and I want to share them, I cannot help but feel the same kind of fears I had when I first started reading Le Guin in English. For example, I am terrified as I write this because I do not want to make mistakes. I do not want my words to be dismissed because my use of language is not near perfection. I do not wish for people to think that I am breaking something I have tried to reconstruct instead. But I want my mended English to be better than silence. Because, like the wizards of Earthsea, I want to use this other language I learned to make magic.

As a writer of genres that are open to diverse themes, plural worlds, extraterrestrial and nonhuman communication, conlangs, and made-up words, I constantly wonder about the openness of our communities to that same kind of linguistic diversity in its creators. I have seen folks—who are marginalized in other ways—making fun of people for pronouncing a word in an unusual way; well-intentioned readers who expect bilingual authors to create bilingual stories or characters that are "just enough" of a certain ethnicity.

If words are our matter, to reference Le Guin once more, let us create a new world with a new language.

I wonder what would be needed for us to understand and embrace that English, as any living language, is constantly evolving and enriching itself due to its speakers—no matter where they are from or what is their linguistic background. If

2. "Exophony is the practice of (normally creative) writing in a language that is not one's mother tongue." (https://en.wikipedia.org/wiki/Exophony)

we want to nurture an openly diverse community, we need to welcome the other and make it our own. This growing creature made out of signs and sounds, syntax and grammar, form and meaning, is only more beautiful when it is cared for by everyone, when its scars are tended but not erased. That creature of words is whole and never broken.

In my day-to-day life in the US, I cannot go out of my apartment building without hearing at least four languages spoken. Surrounded by other immigrants, people from different diasporas, locals, and folks from other cities, I know that we are all recreating the language we have borrowed from our new home.

I know I am not alone.

Brokenness, to me, sounds like a state of finality. Mending is a constant process, a work of love and care over time, an endeavor of the heart, magic. My mended English, like my fiction, is in constant change. It grows.

Imagine that you now serve the most delicious food in your mended bowl, which shows brilliant, colorful scars where there were once cracks. It is so uniquely yours that it makes you feel that everything in it tastes better.

Imagine other folks here and there in faraway lands fixing their own cracked bowls because they too can mend what should not be broken in the first place.

Nelly Geraldine García-Rosas was born and raised in Mexico but immigrated to the US several years ago. She is a graduate of the Clarion West Writers Workshop class of 2019. Her short fiction has appeared in *Lightspeed*, *Nightmare*, *Strange Horizons*, the World Fantasy Award-winning anthology *She Walks in Shadows*, and elsewhere. She can be found online at nellygeraldine.com and on Twitter as @ kitsune_ng.

So, You Want to Be a Speculative Fiction Writer ...

P. Djèlí Clark

Captain America pulls up a chair, sits down, and looks directly into the camera. "So, you want to be a speculative fiction writer." Then he proceeds to offer you some advice.

I could have used something like this when I first got it in my head that I was going to write speculative fiction, sometime after I graduated college. I had never taken a creative writing course. Hadn't been to a single workshop. If you'd asked me what SFWA was, I'd have guessed perhaps an insurance company.

What qualified me to think I could even write genre? The answer was simple. I'd grown up reading and watching all forms of speculative fiction. I was versed in the lore. It was in my veins. Throughout my childhood, I'd devoured speculative fiction that barely included anyone who looked like me. I was determined to provide a corrective: to create a fantasy book with people who resembled me, from cultures that didn't include horse lords and broadswords. I didn't want to supplant those texts. I wanted to add to them. And I wanted it to be grand, on an epic scale. That was enough. Wasn't it?

I dove into writing, carefree and headfirst. I wrote, in copious amounts. With drafts and re-drafts, character sketches and tons of research. I wrote, first one book. Then two. When my massive fantasy tome was completed, I sat back in satisfaction at what had been several years of effort. Then I realized something: I had not a single clue what to do next. I knew absolutely nothing about the publishing world. And I had no guides. All my creativity and storytelling born from reading and watching speculative fiction hadn't prepared me for ... THE INDUSTRY.

— Cue: Dramatic music, followed by thunder and lightning. —

But I wasn't daunted. I went out and got one of those nifty *Guide to Literary Agents* published each year and tried to educate myself on how this whole publishing thing worked. That immediately gave me a massive headache. Agents. Query Letters. Publishers. Slush Piles. And again, what the heck was SFWA?! No one had warned me this was so complicated!

I learned some lessons during this time, sobering ones. One, my precious idea wasn't as unique as I thought. It turned out, there were dozens of people like me, from marginalized backgrounds, who were looking to break the seeming hegemony of Eurocentric fantasy. In fact, there were several successful BIPOC authors who had pioneered that road long before I put fingers to keyboard. Two, writing a book and getting it published are two animals so unrelated they might as well exist on opposite ends of the biological spectrum. The publishing plane was wholly unrelated to my world of plot formation, characters, structures, pacing, and sequences. I had no idea how to approach it. Third, I had not the slightest inkling how to get the attention of any agent, much less a publisher. This was way too hard. I needed a lucky break.

I got one.

A friend of mine worked for a reputable agent, a woman of color whose roster included some well-known authors, academic and literary. She represented nothing in genre, but there was the possibility she might be interested in taking me on as a client. Sparing me the pitch and query process, I was able to pass on my novel to one of this agent's readers. They. Loved. It. The story, the characters, the fact that it was set in this very different fantasy realm. They pushed it onto the agent and before I could exclaim, "Great Caesar's Contract!" I had an agent. And I lived happily ever after.

Not.

There was more educating to be had. The agent saw my two-book novels and immediately informed me, as one would a child, "These are of Biblical proportions. You won't attract a publisher until you cut this down to something manageable." Lengths for books? Shelf space? Those were things? It was a welcome learning moment. I did research to ascertain the proper lengths and the two books became four, with the first at a humble and respectable "debut author" length. After some further edits and some hacking and cutting, that first book was ready to be sent out!

And face rejection.

Rejections can come in all types. There are the ones that disappoint because they read like a rote template. Others that make you wince because they hit at your tender spots. Then there are those that leave you frustrated because they're so bizarre you wonder if your book was read at all.

Looking back in hindsight, I realize I made enough of my own blunders: story openings without that essential hook; overly wordy beginnings; events that didn't immediately move the plot. I also got another life lesson. Somehow, in all my studies and understandings of race and difference, I had placed my fantasy work above all that. Yes, I knew genre was not very diverse at the time. That's one reason I'd picked up the pen. But somehow, I'd convinced myself it was because they hadn't seen what I had to offer yet. Hubris and youth. I was quickly forced to accept a profound truth: diversity in genre wasn't rare because others hadn't tried. I would later hear tales of many who had tried, only to come up against an impenetrable wall minded by gatekeepers with limited imaginations of what genre could be.

Finally, however, I got a bite. A Black imprint, run by a larger publishing house, liked my novel! Two editors there were eager to break into the speculative fiction market. I was informed they would have a meeting to pitch it and that there were high hopes. I couldn't believe it. This was finally going to happen!

Wasn't it?

Ever heard of the American footballer Kevin Dyson who got tackled just short of a touchdown at Superbowl XXXIV? That's about how I felt when the imprint got back to me saying they hadn't been able to get a unanimous vote. While everyone liked the story and the idea, even a Black imprint was uncertain how my fantasy series would fare in a mainstream publishing world where faces like mine remained uncommon. Like Dyson getting tackled at that Superbowl back in 2000, I learned the hard way that in this game of inches, there's no such thing as almost.

So, the novel went back out. And the rejections piled up. After a while, I didn't hear much from my agent. Then without warning, I was informed she was folding up shop. I was released from my contract and that was that. About then, I decided I'd had just about enough of this writing thing. Me and writing needed a formal separation. I took my grand epic fantasy, set it in a box, and stuffed it away like in that scene of the government warehouse in *Raiders of the Lost Ark*. And after a while, I just didn't write at all.

Then, about two years later, I joined an online collective of Black science fiction writers, artists, and creators. My mind was blown. Here were people who looked like me doing so many different projects. And we all had somewhat similar stories. They had grown up on genre too. They all found its lack of diversity unfulfilling. They were all driven to change that.

Inspired, I decided to try my hand at writing again, a novelette-length fantasy piece called *Skin Magic*, and I posted it in a series of blogs on the site. Set in a fictional African Sahel, it follows a thief cursed with tattoos that are a portal to otherworldly horrors. Author Milton J. Davis, who I met on the site, noticed the story and brought it to the attention of the late Charles Saunders—the literal father of modern Black fantasy, or "Sword and Soul" as he called it, and ...

Hold up. You don't know about Charles Saunders? Sword and Soul? Okay.

— *Cue: Flashback sequence, fades to black and white.* —

In the 1970s, African American (and later Afro-Canadian) writer Charles Saunders began publishing short fantasy stories in small magazine presses. Saunders, who had grown up reading Edgar Rice Burroughs' Tarzan novels and Robert E. Howard's *Conan*, struck upon the idea of writing fantasy during the heady political 1960s—in part due to the heightened race consciousness about identity and Africa during the Black Protest movements. His stories pulled on African history, as opposed to, as he put it, "the usual Celtic, Arthurian and Scandinavian underpinnings" that dominated modern fantasy. "I saw a need," Saunders would later claim, "and believed I could fulfill it." This led to his ground-breaking *Imaro* saga set in a precolonial African-inspired fantasy world of heroes, monsters, and magic.

Saunders passed away in 2020. But his legacy was profound.

In 2011, Saunders collaborated with Milton J. Davis, author of the African-based *Meji* fantasy saga, to co-edit a volume of writings called *Griots: A Sword and Soul Anthology*. Saunders had coined the term "Sword and Soul" sometime after 2005 to make the sub-genre distinct from the Euro-dominated "Sword and Sorcery." It was as both were putting together this first-of-its-kind anthology that I completed my short story *Skin Magic*. Milton Davis showed it to Charles, who liked it. THE Charles Saunders liked my writing! He really, really liked it! Both asked me to be part of the upcoming anthology. I said yes, of course! I had never read or heard of Saunders or Davis until well into adulthood. But like them, I was driven by the same glaring lack they had identified decades earlier. I wanted to see fantasy in worlds populated with people and cultures that looked more like me—and less like Scandinavian horse lords.

Charles Saunders had literally saved my speculative fiction writing life.

— *End flashback scene.* —

So, that's how I returned to writing again.

This time though, I had more humble aspirations. Instead of epic tomes, I focused on short stories. I began learning and really researching this market of genre I was trying to break into.

I even learned what SFWA was. What was more, I began reading a lot of short stories. I immersed myself in the genre I loved to help me better understand the techniques of short-storytelling. And to just enjoy some good writing! It took some practice and imagination to pull off my own stories. But after a few tries, and some steady rejections, I managed to get a few published: in pro and semipro markets. In time, I would have my own books. And a chance to join SFWA. It had been a long journey with unexpected turns, but it happened.

So, what lessons did I learn? Things take time. Breaking into the writing biz took a lot longer than I'd hoped. And there's absolutely nothing wrong with that. Can't say I've grown to love rejections, which I still get. But they're a part of this writing life. Grow from them if you can and try not to take them to heart. I also learned that sometimes, success is just dumb luck. In 2015, I put out a call on Facebook asking if anyone knew a place where I could publish a 12,000-word novelette about a dandy-dressing lady detective set in an alternative turn-of-the-century Cairo, filled with steampunk and magic. By chance, an editor at Tor.com noticed my post. She inquired and, yadda, yadda, yadda ... that's how my story, "A Dead Djinn in Cairo" got published, opening a lot of doors. That wasn't anything I could have planned. I just had the random fortune to be in the right place at the right time. What I learned from that was, keep putting your stuff out there—because you never know who's looking.

My last lesson takes me back to that almost-published fantasy series from my past. Sometimes getting published (or not) is about forces beyond our control, our abilities to write, or our imagination. They are systemic. There are stories I've published today which I'm almost certain would not have gotten another look ten years ago. That an editor at Tor.com (a woman of color) was minding the gates and *actively* seeking more diverse voices was, without doubt, instrumental in my story being published.

The genre isn't the same as when I first started out. Not perfect by any means. True diversity and equity remain a work in progress. But at least now, voices long ignored are being heard.

The very insular landscape of SFF publishing has shifted, making it a more accessible space. Editors and agents now hang out on Twitter. It no longer feels like the impenetrable wall I encountered starting out two decades past.

How long will this era of calls for diversity and openness last? Who can say. There's certainly a backlash from among some sectors of the genre community who are certain that while talking dragons can exist in their fantasy world, Black and Brown people cannot. Thankfully, those reactionaries don't speak for most of the fanbase, who represent an increasingly diverse and global community. As long as that trend continues, the industry will likely continue to support new and different voices. But I'm not in the predicting business. History can move backwards as well as forwards. Up to us to see that its trajectory bends inevitably towards justice.

So, what about that grand fantasy tome? The one that was *almost* published? The one that perhaps might get a fairer hearing today? It's still sitting in that warehouse with Indiana Jones's Ark of the Covenant. Maybe I'll return to it one day. Maybe. In the meantime, I got new worlds to dream up and new stories to write.

Phenderson Djéli Clark is the author of the novel A *Master of Djinn*, and the award-winning and Hugo, Nebula, World Fantasy, and Sturgeon nominated author of the novellas *Ring Shout*, *The Black God's Drums*, and *The Haunting of Tram Car 015*. His short stories have appeared in online venues such as Tor.com, *Heroic Fantasy Quarterly*, *Beneath Ceaseless Skies*, and in print anthologies including *Hidden Youth* and *Black Boy Joy*.

Everything Else Is on Hold

S.B. Divya

In November 2021, I spent half a day at San Diego Comic-Con's Special Edition. I was on a discussion panel, and then I signed some books. It was my first large in-person event since the COVID pandemic, and I was really nervous about attending, but not for the reasons you might think.

In January 2021, during the peak winter surge of COVID-19 in California, I went to the grocery store to buy a cake for the presidential inauguration. I wore a cloth mask and gloves. Four days later, I developed a sore throat and a low fever, and I tested positive for COVID.

For two weeks, I isolated myself in my bedroom. My spouse delivered food on a tray outside my closed door. I used FaceTime to talk to him and our child. Our cats were very confused. Thankfully, no one else in my family got sick. I went through many of the typical symptoms—fever, body aches, loss of smell, mild shortness of breath—but I recovered. My oxygen levels were fine. I didn't end up in the hospital. My nose started working again after three weeks. All things considered, I got off easy.

Four weeks after I tested positive, I went on a half-mile hike. I developed some chest pressure after and was advised to lay off the exercise for a while. A couple of weeks later, my first novel, *Machinehood*, was published. My time and energy were consumed with promoting my book and all the excitement of being a debut author. My chest pain eased, and I gradually ramped up my activity with gentle yoga and short walks. By mid-April, I felt fine.

Then came the weekend when I was a guest of honor at a virtual convention. I was thrilled, of course, and glad to participate as much as I could. I spent hours on Zoom doing panels and other live interactions. Three days later, I found myself too weak to stand while preparing dinner. My heart pounded. My chest hurt. I felt nauseated. I thought I was having a heart attack, except that it lasted for hours.

A trip to urgent care showed a clean ECG and chest X-ray. My regular doctor had nothing to add. Rather than going straight to a long list of expensive specialists, I looked into COVID recovery clinics. The one at Cedars-Sinai in Los Angeles had a six-month waitlist. Luckily, another had just opened at UC Irvine. There, I found a doctor who listened and understood my symptoms (far too many people in my situation are dismissed as having panic attacks or anxiety). They ran me through a comprehensive set of tests. The only medically noticeable problem they found was a mild reduction in gas exchange in my lungs. The ultimate diagnosis: the syndrome often called "long COVID." The doctor handed me some pamphlets on myalgic encephalomyelitis (ME—sometimes referred to as chronic fatigue syndrome), pacing, and managing my "energy envelope."

I've had to deal with various physical impediments for much of my life, but they've all been treatable in some fashion. Glasses and contact lenses for my severe myopia. Enzyme pills for lactose intolerance. Botox, pain meds, and trigger avoidance for chronic migraines. I've made lifestyle changes to mitigate jaw dysfunction and acid reflux problems.

Prior to having intraocular lenses implanted in my eyes (yes, I'm a cyborg now), I couldn't see past my nose without correction. It was a rule in our household to never move my glasses, so I'd always know where to find them, even while blind. I worried about how I'd fare during a midnight emergency or an apocalypse, and that anxiety has shaped some of my fiction. I like writing stories about people who aren't typical heroes—people who have some form of illness or disability, people who come from underprivileged social classes, people who struggle to be seen as protagonists in their own lives.

In two strokes of irony, I've written characters whose health problems ended up being similar to mine. In *Machinehood*, the character Welga Ramírez develops neurological problems but continues to work and push herself too hard. I wrote the first draft of that novel in 2017, and in 2018, I developed chronic migraines in parallel with starting a new job, teaching coding to elementary school kids, and revising my novel. My family pointed out that I was pushing too hard, just like Welga.

In *Meru*, my novel coming in 2023, the character Jayanthi has sickle cell disease, which means she has issues with physical endurance as well as periodic health crises, especially in times of stress. I wrote this far-future space opera in 2020 as a form of mental release from the isolation and stress of the pandemic. A year later, I developed my own chronic illness and disability, and while I could sympathize with Jayanthi before, I can relate to her now.

I spent much of the summer of 2021 reading, experimenting, and learning about ME and how to manage it. I started wearing a Fitbit and religiously tracking my steps. I set a low heart rate threshold to track my stress and activity. According to the CDC's COVID-19 science update from September 2020, there's some indication that the disease can reduce a person's VO_2 max, which measures the maximum rate of oxygen consumption during exercise of increasing intensity. I tried to figure out what my limits were, and at what rate I could increase them without triggering another relapse. It took four months to go from 2,000 steps per day to 3,500, but then a "crash," or relapse, kept me from progressing further.

Ordinary activities that I used to take for granted—showering, washing dishes, laundry, sitting upright, talking—now make me tired. My heart rate varies depending on my posture, diet, and stress levels. Multimodal activities like video games or Zoom chats are even worse. I can't even contemplate hiking, biking, travel, or many of the other activities I used to love. Thankfully, I can still work, but brain effort translates into fatigue as well, and I can only manage two or three hours a day, whereas before, I was able to juggle three jobs (writing, engineering, and editing *Escape Pod*) and eight to ten productive hours a day.

My family and friends kept hoping that after I got my vaccinations, or after some time and rest, I'd improve. I did, too, which is why I didn't speak publicly about my condition for the first eight months. Unfortunately, the opposite happened. My constellation of symptoms increased over time. Extended inactivity made me weak. Physical therapy gave me persistent muscle aches. Off-label medication had no effect.

I'd hoped that I understood my limits well enough to handle the exertion of San Diego Comic-Con. It was within an hour's driving distance. I wasn't planning to do anything resembling my usual level of convention activity, and this Special Edition version was uncrowded and easy compared to pre-pandemic versions. I allowed myself plenty of time to walk slowly, rest, eat, and stay hydrated.

It wasn't enough. After avoiding a relapse for four months, I ended up spending several days lying on the couch, exhausted, achy, and unable to do anything other than the essentials (eating, sleeping, childcare). I fell behind on nearly two weeks' worth of work.

I had planned to attend the 79th World Science Fiction Convention (also known as WorldCon) a few weeks later, in December, in Washington, DC. I was really looking forward to seeing friends, colleagues, and fans and to attending the Hugo Award Ceremony as a double nominee. It would have been my first time flying since the pandemic started. I've always loved to travel, and with each WorldCon being hosted by a different city every year, it provided a great excuse.

Unfortunately, my experience in San Diego made it clear that attending WorldCon would be a massive detriment to my health. Talking loudly (a necessity while wearing a mask) makes my lungs ache. Walking across one airport terminal is equivalent to my full daily step count. Being mindful of my energy levels would mean saying no to three quarters of the activities I'd want to do. Add in the latest COVID variant, the reports of angry anti-maskers on airplanes, the dearth of taxi drivers, and learning to navigate wheelchair access for air travel, it was simply too much. I canceled my trip.

Was I disappointed? Of course! It's hard watching friends and colleagues having a good time without me. It's hard when my family goes hiking or biking or snowboarding ... without me. But I can't keep living as if good health is around the corner.

A year has passed since I first got sick, eight months since my first big relapse. As I write this, long COVID can't be treated, avoided, or cured for most people. This is no longer an illness. It's not transient. It's not a thing that gradually resolves over time. It's a chronic disease, recognized as a disability by the US government, with periods of remission and relapse that could last for the rest of my life. What I have is here to stay.

Like many chronic diseases, it's a condition whose severity waxes and wanes. From the reading I've done and the people I've spoken to, living with long-term disability is often a process of learning how to unwind from expectations, set realistic goals, and maintain good habits. It can take years to understand your limits and then to gradually rebuild your life. Ordinary illnesses are amplified. Daily rest is a necessity. You're always at risk of pushing too hard too fast and falling into a relapse, sometimes after years of feeling at full health. I've spent the past year experiencing and internalizing this.

On the plus side—such as it is—this not a progressive condition like Parkinson's (as far as we can tell). The bottom line might not get worse if I take care of myself. And because of the sheer number of people affected by long COVID, real money is going into researching the problem—unlike ME, which has been neglected for decades. Maybe in a few years, we'll understand both disorders better. Maybe at some point in my lifetime, we'll have a proven treatment.

In the meantime, I focus on the things I can do: write books and stories (slowly), drive my kid to school, eat, shower, do the laundry. I'll work on gradually rebuilding my strength at a pace that my body will tolerate. I'll keep my socializing short, take road trips where I can lie down across the back seat, and prioritize my health above all else. I should eventually have periods of remission, perhaps lasting for years. Until then, everything else is on hold.

If you'd like to donate to research on ME and long COVID, visit the Solve ME/CFS Initiative at solvecfs.org.

S.B. Divya (she/any) is a lover of science, math, fiction, and the Oxford comma. She is the Hugo and Nebula nominated author of *Meru* (2023), *Machinehood*, *Runtime*, and *Contingency Plans For the Apocalypse and Other Possible Situations*. Her short stories have appeared in numerous magazines and anthologies, and she was the co-editor of Escape Pod, the weekly science fiction podcast, 2017–2022. Divya holds degrees in Computational Neuroscience and Signal Processing, and she worked for twenty years as an electrical engineer before becoming an author. Born in Pondicherry, India, Divya now resides in Southern California. She enjoys subverting expectations and breaking stereotypes whenever she can. Find out more about her at www.sbdivya.com or on Twitter as @divyastweets.

Forever a Work in Progress
On Writing and Transition

Sagan Yee

Five years ago, if you had asked friends and colleagues what kind of a writer I was, they would probably have cited my meticulously detailed work emails and grant applications. I'd spent most of the last decade as a community organizer and nonprofit administrator, primarily in the indie video games sector. Though my laptop is filled with thousands of words of fiction—enough to fill a couple of good-sized novels—it's only recently that any of them have begun to see the light of day.

So what am I doing in this anthology, among "Real Authors," some of whom have even had their work printed on "Real Paper"? To put it simply: Chinelo asked me.

Chinelo was my mentor at Clarion West, the Seattle-based workshop for writers of speculative fiction which I attended virtually in 2021. When she asked me to contribute to this anthology, I very nearly said no. My internal reasoning was that I wasn't ready yet. At the time she made the offer, I hadn't had any work published. I hadn't made a name for myself. My outdated website had no indication that writing fiction was even something I did, and so on and so forth ...

Eventually, I realized how silly this was. Here was an editor inviting me to write about my personal struggles with gender identity and artistic authenticity, and I was preparing to turn down the offer because I didn't think I was worthy of being included. Every amazing opportunity I've had in life started with someone insisting

I could do it, that I was meant to be there, that my voice needed to be heard. Perhaps I'd forgotten that. Or maybe I was balking at the prospect of having to write about that most difficult and mysterious of subjects: Myself.

I'd once met up with friends from out of town. They'd invited another acquaintance whom I'd never met, and one friend introduced me as: "This is Sagan. They're a science-fiction writer."

I laughed, brushing it off. Later, over brunch, I mentioned offhandedly that I was between careers, and that I had no idea what I was going to do next. This same friend said, with supreme confidence, "Of course you do. You're going to be a super famous author, right?" When I stared blankly, they added, "It's okay, you don't have to believe us. We'll do the believing for you."

These are the kind of declarative statements made not as fact, but as prophecy. But the nature of a prophecy is that—like a wish granted by a sarcastic genie—it never fulfills itself in a straightforward or easy way. There's always a twist. And because this is the real world, the twist may be that the prophecy doesn't come to pass at all.

"Writer" is not the only label I struggle with accepting. "Man" is another. I often wonder if I am running away from something by choosing to identify as nonbinary, rather than as male. When strangers address me as "sir" or when other men do that curt little head-bob as they pass me coming out of the men's washroom, I do not correct their assumption. When I walk into a bar with a cisgendered male friend and the server greets us with: "What can I get you gentlemen?" I feel simultaneously elated and afraid. As if at any moment, they will realize their mistake and take it back.

For those of us who identify as some flavor of transmasculine nonbinary, there is a common tendency to reject the term "man"—preferring adjacent descriptors like "guy," "dude," or "bro." "Man" in the context of a greeting, as in: "Hey man," can be acceptable. But the glaring binarism of ticking M as opposed to F on the gender options of a passport or a medical form feels wrong. The possible reasons for this discomfort are as diverse as transmasculinity itself: The baggage associated with cishet macho culture, the unpleasant strictures of Western notions of manhood. Sometimes it just doesn't "feel right," like a too-tight pair of shoes.

I wonder if there are similar methods of evasion that I can employ the next time someone introduces me as a "future famous author"? Anything to take the pressure off. What is the equivalent of "guy" for a practitioner of the literary arts? "Dabbler" perhaps? Or "dilettante." Guys revel in their guy-ness, but they're not too serious about it. They don't feel the need to attend conferences or six-week workshops to learn about guyhood. They simply *are*, in a way I could never be.

Writer. Man. Other people have earned the right to call themselves such things after they've come out with one or two bestselling novels and grown a proper beard. But not me. I still have a long way to go. And are beards and bestsellers even things that I want? Is that all there is at the end of the rainbow, the last stop on an inevitable trajectory of medicalized transition and professional ambition?

If I struggle with questions of authenticity, it is because society does not hold space for things it sees as in-between, undefined, or liminal. We lack the language to acknowledge the power of that which exists beyond labels, forgetting that not all who wander are lost. Being nonbinary is not a milestone on the way to some specific destination. Nonbinariness forms its own geography, constitutes a territory unto itself. Our boundaries may be fluid, but just because we can't be mapped doesn't mean we don't exist. We live in a society so ready to put the squeeze on anyone who doesn't fit into a preconceived box that it can be easier to crush desire into denial—as easy as crushing coal into a diamond. Which is to say, not easy at all. Not without the application of extreme pressure.

᠊ᢀᢀᢀ᠊

Why is it so important to me to draw parallels between my writing and being trans? It is not an immediately intuitive connection, nor a universally resonant one. Writing is a craft, a set of skills that can be honed through exercise and persistence. Calling oneself a writer implies a dedication to a profession or vocation. In contrast, transness (for lack of a better word) is often described as a *condition*. Much of our struggle involves convincing others that being trans is an integral part of our identity, not a choice.

But my experience of being trans is filled with choices. In fact, much of the fatigue and joy of transness comes from the sheer number of decisions, large and small, that I am faced with every day. Should I bind my breasts? Stick a rolled-up pair of socks down my pants? Start a GoFundMe for top surgery? Do I correct people when they use the wrong pronouns, or let it slide? Where should I get my hair cut? Which bathroom do I use? Or do I do nothing, and hope these never-ending questions go away on their own?

This progress by slow increments closely mirrors what it feels like to self-edit my own stories. I cut here, add there. I alter one sentence at a time, each small step bringing the piece closer to realizing itself. The core idea never changes, but it develops and become stronger, clearer. To me, gender transition is the process of editing my own story.

Every week, I stick a needle in my leg and fill my body with masculinizing drugs. Every week, I sit down at the keyboard and fill the screen with words from my imagination. Both acts are intimate, private. I do these things for my own gratification, to affirm my personal sense of "rightness." At the same time however, these acts are not only for myself. Some of it is for you: the invisible, hoped-for audience. Performing gender and creating art are both an expression, however incremental or flawed, of my inner self.

For this purpose, I find writing to be preferable to the many other mediums—animation, video games, cinema—in which I've plied my trade. They all have so many moving parts and technical hoops to jump through before the art can be called complete. Any of these filters can dilute the artist's message, rendering it less personal by the time it gets to its destination. In comparison, committing words to page requires so little extraneous equipment or involvement from other people that the bridge between the artist's self and their audience is that much shorter. As far as raw expression goes, writing is as close to the bone as it gets.

But this vulnerability cuts both ways. With writing, it's difficult to hide your predilections and fascinations—your biases and obsessions—from the reader. Or from yourself. Was returning to writing in 2018, a year before I came out, the catalyst for realizing I was trans? Or a harbinger?

⁘

On my hard drive live unpublished tales of ancient, primordial fish and godlike nanobot sludge, genetically engineered theme park mascots, and a woman so obsessed with a good hot sauce that she just might kill for it. I've written about plant people and bird people and people who secrete intelligence-boosting drugs from their head tentacles. I write about cyborgs who fear a memory reset, spaceships with gambling problems, and slipstream assassins who fall in love. Do I really want to write about "the queer trans Chinese-Canadian experience?"

Growing up, White Cishet Masculinity was my version of Middle Earth. It was a fantastical place I could escape to any time I wanted, as simultaneously real and not-real as anything dreamed up by Tolkien. Although I didn't question my Assigned Gender at Birth until my early thirties, as a teen I had trouble reading books where the protagonist was described using she/her pronouns. I couldn't relate, couldn't envision myself in the role.

I remember spending a lot of time in the General Fiction section of the public library, where they kept all the grown-up books about murder and middle-aged crises. "Men in their forties and fifties having affairs" was a subject that I specifically sought out when perusing the jacket blurbs. I pored over the likes of Irving, Updike, Burgess, and Murakami. If I wasn't engrossed in stories about men struggling with baldness and erectile dysfunction, I was eating up the kiss-kiss-bang-bang classic genre pulp of Ian Fleming's James Bond series, or the hard-boiled detective tales by Dashiell Hammett and Raymond Chandler.

Even then, I knew this was weird. Except for my hatred of dresses and skirts, I wasn't a sporty tomboy. I had no problem being thought of as a bookish, nerdy Asian girl. I simply, for whatever reason, gravitated towards stories where (usually) white men had violent adventures and sometimes cheated on their wives. I didn't have the critical capacity to understand why these books held so much dangerous appeal.

Having come out recently—just a few years before this essay was written—I can now approach these problematic faves with a little more understanding. It wasn't the content of these books that interested me so much as the distance involved. Despite what I consider to be a pretty fantastic upbringing on the part of my parents and siblings, some part of me always knew I wasn't exactly what I'd been told I was. So, I overcompensated. I was attracted to stories that would let me dissociate into perspectives as seemingly far removed from my own as possible: Straight White Maleness as escapism.

Now that I've rediscovered my own sense of masculinity, I am interested in telling my version of it. This involves the long, slow work of coming back into myself, of being able to see the world through my own eyes and create art with my own mind. I once saw a fanfic on Archive of Our Own with the custom tag "the mortifying ordeal of being known," a quote-turned-meme from a 2013 essay by Tim Kreider. It stuck with me. Only recently have I been able to admit that I have a fear of being seen. And this fear has impacted my writing.

Our first instructor at Clarion West, Andy Duncan, led us through a writing exercise. It was a simple prompt: Write about the strangest thing that's ever happened to you. After reading some of the results out loud, he said that students often struggle with writing their own lived experiences. They try to embellish the narrative, jazz it up, all too aware of their audience's perceived need to be entertained.

I don't think this problem is unique to writers of science fiction and fantasy. I've read plenty of "literary" fiction that rings false, attempting to fulfill someone else's expectations. It is entirely possible to write about aliens and spaceships from a place of personal truth, or to write a memoir that obfuscates more than it illuminates. Self-expression is not the same as self-disclosure. And it's impossible to make art honestly, in any medium, when you don't know yourself.

In my case, Andy was absolutely right. After his lesson, I tried a few new things. I wrote about gender and sex and building community and what it means to be from a particular place and time. I wrote a story set in the suburbs of the Canadian prairies, where the only points of interest within walking distance of the protagonist's house are a Blockbuster and a public library. I put blue tentacled aliens there, too. They are just as real as anything else that's ever happened to me.

This essay, being somewhat devoid of telepathic spiders and vampiric app developers, was one of the most difficult things I've ever written. As a reward, I wanted to make this final section a space for intentionality, a set of promises to myself.

I'm going to challenge myself to write about things I find uncomfortable or don't fully understand, things I want to see more of in the world, and things I want the world to better understand about me. And I'll continue to write about robot gods and time traps, noir VR idols and whatever random thing I overheard on the subway last Thursday. I'll keep submitting stories to literary markets I admire. I want to finish a novel. I want to attend a writing conference in person. I'm going to get my work out there, not for fame or glory, but to practice being seen.

I've theorized that returning to writing was somehow the key to realizing something long-buried about my gender identity. I'm interested to see what else I'll discover as I continue to deepen my craft. Like the early months of taking testosterone, I anticipate the changes will not be apparent at first. Some may be so glacial as to appear static. That's okay. The trick is to take it one step at a time.

Strangers look at my short haircut and chin fuzz and call me "sir," and I nod politely and smile. Others will read the words I've written and propel me to literary stardom or—more than likely—not, and either will be just fine. I'll accept labels when they feel useful and discard them when they don't. I will embrace the undefinable. I will remain forever a work in progress.

Sagan Yee is a nonbinary media artist and organizer based in Treaty 13 territory, Tkaronto (Toronto, Canada). Their creative practice includes animation, speculative fiction, screen-based digital games, playful experiences, and alternative controller collaborations. They are the former Executive Director of Hand Eye Society, a nonprofit video game arts organization, and a Clarion West 2021 graduate. You can find them online at www.saganyee.com.

Exposition Tax
The hidden burden of writing from the margins

Suyi Davies Okungbowa

I read the first of the Harry Potter books as a teenager, long before the author became the divisive figure she is today. Back then, I had heard all the buzz about them, but as a youngster living in Benin City, Nigeria, could not convince my parents to splash a quarter of the national minimum wage on a book. So, when a classmate offered me a bootleg copy (I did not ask where she got it), I was excited. I dove into the world of No. 4 Privet Drive. I followed Harry's strange and enthralling encounters in the muggle world, right up to the point at the train station, where he slips through to Platform 9¾ and into the world of wizardry.

"What's a platform?" I remember asking myself.

See, my ancient city did not have trains, and at this point I'd never traveled out of it. My only reference so far had been images in books and on TV. I knew what trains and train tracks and train stations looked like, but for the life of me, I did not understand how a platform fit into all this. There was no Google at the time—or at least it wasn't as accessible as it is right now—so I dove for the next best thing: a dictionary. Though I found the definition of a platform there, I did not find a fitting explanation for how Harry Potter could push a cart full of school supplies through "a flat, raised area or structure."

It did not cross the mind of the author to explain how platforms at a train station function. This is "common knowledge," you might say, something the "majority of readers" should be aware of. Therein lies an unspoken decision: that any reader who doesn't understand train stations might as well suck it up and find out for themselves.

Consider this same scenario, but instead, let's reverse the roles. Say the author is Nigerian and references something commonplace but particular to African cities—for example, the commercial minibus called danfo in Lagos, tuke-tuke in Benin City, trotro in Accra, and matatu in Nairobi. (I bet you're running off to Google now, wondering what these look like.) Now imagine if said author made a feature typical of these kinds of vehicles— for example, the large drum subwoofers often fitted into the back—important to visualizing a story. Fascinating, yes? But not to the author, who witnesses this every day and so expects their primary audience and the "majority of readers" to understand without further exposition.

Imagine the kerfuffle.

What actually happens is that the Nigerian author will consider that perhaps the "majority of readers" are neither Nigerian nor from Benin City (even if their primary audience is), and therefore may have never seen such a vehicle, to talk less of being in one. So, they will offer a few lines of description and/or explanation to help the reader visualize it. Better, right?

But it isn't just that one scene, is it? Now they have to do this for a whole story or book. At every point in the narrative where there is the slightest possibility that a reader outside of the author's primary sociocultural context could be yanked out of the story by a lack of understanding, they must provide explanation and nuance, both of which require exposition through narrative, dialogue, and other forms. Eventually, their story will possess much more exposition than those of authors from more culturally dominant parts of the world. And readers who have been raised on a diet of stories from those culturally dominant places will find themselves unsettled by this. When someone asks them if they enjoyed the story, they will say, "Yes, but ..." But it was weird. But it was a lot. But it was different. But, but, but.

Congratulations, dear reader. You have just witnessed the exposition tax in action.

The double consciousness of the marginalized writer.

Let's start again, from the beginning.

One of the first assumptions this essay makes is that you, the reader, knows what *Harry Potter* is, that you've read the first book or seen the first movie. It even assumes you know what a platform looks like. It assumes a lot of things about you before you even arrive at the page.

This is the thing every reader must understand: stories, by default, make assumptions about their readers. About what they may not know and must be told, what they *should* know and therefore don't have to be told, and what may be safely withheld, to be divulged later in the narrative for maximum impact. Every story, by its very telling, paints a profile of its reader. While not every reader who understands and enjoys the story will fit this profile, an overlap of identity, interests, and experiences is often required to fully engage with it.

For example, a storyteller's culture informs how they structure their story, what references they invoke, what narrative styles and patterns they lean into, and what tropes they employ. If a significant amount of the storyteller's readership also comes from their cultural space, it creates a feedback loop: *the storyteller's approach builds the reader's expectations, which informs the storyteller's approach, which builds the reader's expectations.* If the storytellers and readers within this feedback loop come from a culturally dominant space, then readers from outside this space will either have to accept these stories and their manner of telling as the norm—or be shut out.

When telling their own tales, storytellers outside of these culturally dominant spaces—those from the margins, if you will—now have to decide how much of these dominant forms and approaches they want to keep and how much they would like to reinvent, subvert, or discard. Unfortunately, keeping dominant forms might mean that whatever story they tell—whether representative of their identity and lived experience or not— will carry the timbre of those forms. These storytellers also risk adopting the unexamined assumptions and approaches inherent in those forms, especially those descended from colonial and imperialist traditions, such as Orientalist and Othering language. So, while readers who are conversant with the dominant forms and approaches will recognize them, marginalized writers are forced to twist themselves into shoes that pinch.

The second option is to present the story in a way that is as true as possible to their marginalized self and lived experience. This means employing language, structure, voice, form, and approach that mark the story as proud of its own heritage. But now they must contend with readers from the dominant space—and there will be a significant number of them—who may find it difficult to accept this approach, or are outright unwilling to.

This double consciousness is a burden every storyteller from the margins—especially writers—must bear. It weighs on us with every story we tell. Over and over and over we ask: *How much is too much? How little is too little?* Where writers from dominant spaces can spend time honing their craft with abandon, we must work with one eye on balance. Not in service of ourselves or our stories, but for the sake of the voices that have the ears of the storytelling ecosystem.

Writing like the majority, reading like the minority.
In an interview with *The Daily Trojan*, the online student newspaper of the University of Southern California, Vietnamese-American writer and professor Viet Thanh Nguyen offers some advice to authors facing this dilemma:

> If you are coming from a background outside of [the majority] as some kind of disempowered, marginalized, minority population, you may feel the pressure to explain yourself and your culture, to translate yourself, your languages, your customs, and so on and so forth—this is something that must be absolutely resisted by any writer. When I say write like a majority, I don't mean like a white person, I mean write as if we ourselves are speaking to ourselves, and let

everyone else catch up. That's where you get interesting art, and even hopefully, great art, to come from (Stuart Carson, "Write Like You Are the Majority," *Daily Trojan*, October 21, 2020).

Nguyen posits that one must avoid putting oneself under pressure to write *toward* the cultural majority of global readership and focus more on expressing one's experiences as deftly as possible. The ideal scenario would be for the writer to err on the side of specificity, confident that universality will be found within.

In a fair and just world, this wonderful piece of advice would not be difficult to follow. But given our notoriously unfair and unjust world, marginalized authors attempting this approach could become further marginalized for it. In a publishing industry that also includes editorial, sales, marketing, and publicity, the writer-reader relationship is only one amongst many. And all of these contribute to a writer's reach, readership, and success.

When my debut novel, *David Mogo, Godhunter*, was released, it was met with mixed reactions. One group of readers, reviewers, and critics was excited about reading a novel where the narrative did not follow dominant story structures, but instead employed a repetitive, helical form. They loved the infusion of various languages that demonstrated Lagos's multilingual nature. They loved the interiority of the main character, his challenges and dilemmas. These reviews were gold to me, a young author who had written a story just for himself and had not, at the time, given thought to getting published, much less understood.

But then came the other group, the ones who were put off by the very same things. They absolutely detested the character's interiority, were tripped up by the novel's multilingual-ness, and did not appreciate the helical nature of the narrative. And most importantly, they were ruffled by the lack of exposition of allusions that were unfamiliar to them. I was lucky enough that this lack of enthusiasm did not impact my publishing trajectory. Many others have not been so lucky.

Before I was a professional writer, I was often happy to accept an author's payment of this exposition tax. While I would not always go into a story expecting to be catered to, I often got excited when things were explained for my benefit. It made me feel important that the author did not have me do the extra work of unpacking the cultural subtexts, nuances, and undercurrents existing beyond the surface read.

Feeling centered and important is not, all by itself, a terrible thing. My joy in those instances likely arose from frustration at the paucity of stories that reflected me. But being catered to was not—and still isn't—an expectation, because I was taught to approach each new story as a window to an experience I might not always fully understand.

In his book *Craft In the Real World*, Matthew Salesses discusses craft as "engagement with an audience's bias." A globally dominant readership that is used to being culturally centered eventually develops an expectation that it will always be centered. These expectations then become yardsticks for assessing storytelling craft. And when this is also espoused by a publishing ecosystem most interested in appealing to the lowest common denominator, this practice becomes a self-replicating lie.

Years after my debut, I read the essay "Interrobang and Myth" by Destiny O. Birdsong in *Poetry Magazine*. In it, the poet asks: "Who are you loving when you write?" I finally understood why many authors who write from the margins opt to follow Viet Thanh Nguyen's advice—consequences be damned. Their refusal to pay the exposition tax is a statement of love to the people they wish to center. Writing like the majority is indeed good resistance, and one part of the solution.

The oft-overlooked second part of this solution is learning to read like the minority. Pedagogical practices that offer tools to enable global cultural majorities to approach each work with minimal prejudice can alleviate the burden on the marginalized storyteller. As a professor of creative writing, I consider education in reading practices to be just as important as those in writing. It is the hope that such learning can move from niche to mainstream consciousness, and little by little, erode the increased labor required of marginalized storytellers.

Balance: a false goal.

By the time I was ready to write my next novel, *Son of the Storm*, I believed I had devised a solution to the *David Mogo* "problem" of too little exposition. I would aim for an ideal balance. I would offer significantly more explanations but hold back just enough to avoid over-catering to the global cultural majority, thereby satisfying both dominant and minority readers.

It didn't take me long to realize the folly of that idea. Much like the first novel, this one was inspired by, and rooted in, the experiences of marginalized peoples. It demanded complexity, specificity, and nuance—of its characters and its milieu. Approaching this book with the goal of avoiding the discomfort of dominant readership groups already shook its artistic foundations.

I found it laborious to investigate each paragraph, scene, and line, wondering if "everyone" would understand what I was alluding to. It interfered with the creation process, discouraging risk-taking in favor of a flattened relatability. Midway through writing the book, I abandoned this approach and reverted to only telling what needed to be told as the context demanded it.

The novel has been generally well-received. But, unsurprisingly, there remained those who insisted upon maximized exposition. This time, however, they were countered by another group—those who wanted less of it! I learned a major lesson that all authors learn sooner or later: the idea of balance, a situation where all readers can be pleased, is false.

I learned that the loudest voices for or against any authorial craft choice often insist that it is not the craft choice that irks them. It is the presence of anything *they* don't care for. And if they do not care for it, then its existence isn't justified. This quest for balance, therefore, is not really about satisfying multiple sides of the aisle. It's about erasing every side but those of the dominant voices.

For the marginalized storyteller, whose work is often deemed a representation not just of themselves, but of the communities from which they hail, this is a lose-lose game, rigged at inception. Each failure in this regard is a black mark, resulting in the perpetration of a single story: that the failure of this artist's work represents a failure of all.

I have therefore given up the exposition tax in its entirety, along with its fantasy of balance. In its stead, I have adopted a quest for personal assurance that my work represents itself and its origins as closely as possible. My only litmus test these days is the consideration of accessibility.

The Jamaican author and scholar Kei Miller best put this goal into perspective during a 2019 interview at the Association for Commonwealth Literature and Language Studies conference in New Zealand. "There is beauty [and growth] in realizing that you are not the center of the work," he says to dominant global readership groups. He then compares reading to migration. "Migrate to their center," he adds.

A willingness on the part of the majority to migrate leaves the marginalized writer with only one task: to leave the doors open. Leaving the story just accessible enough for anyone to enter has inclusion woven into its fabric and eschews erasure. Best of all, it allows marginalized artists to be who we are, respects who we are not, and does not require us to be who we don't want to be.

Suyi Davies Okungbowa is a Nigerian author of fantasy, science fiction and general speculative work. His latest novel is *Son of the Storm* (Orbit, 2021), first in the epic fantasy trilogy, The Nameless Republic (*Warrior of the Wind*, second in the trilogy, is forthcoming in 2023). His debut godpunk fantasy novel *David Mogo, Godhunter* (Abaddon, 2019), won the 2020 Nommo Ilube Award for Best Novel. His shorter works have appeared in various periodicals and anthologies and have been nominated for various awards. He earned his MFA in Creative Writing from the University of Arizona, and lives in Ontario, where he is a professor of creative writing at the University of Ottawa. Follow him on Twitter and Instagram at @suyidavies, or via his newsletter, SuyiAfterFive.com.

A Writer's Lament in Seven Stages

Shawn Frazier

I. **Hidden Treasures.** Have you ever tried to communicate in a language that was at odds with your voice? I have. Once, I wanted to divorce myself from my authentic voice. I kept it hidden, though it pounded to be set free. Finally, it escaped. Now, it has found a new home in another writer's imagination. They claimed it and wrote it down before me.

I remember when my muse and my story ideas would sneak up behind me while I wrote. I would hear a whisper, a voice in my ear that would turn into a yell. It would keep me awake at night. With my bed covers pulled over my head, I would press my pillow over my ears to pretend it was not there. I hoped it would leave and allow me to rest.

My muse expressed that the form of writing I toiled with was not how I wished to create. How else am I suppose to write? I needed to be understood. I must place Theme, Structure, and Style above anything. Even myself. Before I emancipate my imagination, I must prove to the guard who patrols the golden gates that I'm worthy.

I've a responsibility to my community. Why, I do care to tell it like it is. I refuse to paper my past. Yet, until the gatekeepers have given me permission, I'll do what I must. Rather than follow my "Intense Obsessions," as Kafka once said, I will create what is safe ... Dilute my language and translate my culture before I print it on any page. Bend and water it down; make it sound logical. Use precise words and tell heartfelt stories that are safe. Where readers can relate and not feel chastised. When I discuss my experiences, I must not ridicule the world for how it has treated me in my years of self-doubt and pain.

My actual vision will be put on paper only when I receive their approval. Otherwise, the gatekeepers will think I've revolted and I'm writing to critique their rules.

2. My Muse. There you are! I haven't seen you for a while. You must have heard me ramble, and tip-toed out the shadows to see. How did you ever get free? Stop that! … Go away. … You've disrupted my ability to discuss race relations and violence. Just go back into the closet with the other ideas I shelved away, with my other rejected fables. … What? You say I play in racial tropes? I think you should have your tongue removed. Stop all that chatter and whispering; I can't think of what I want to compose. … You are a headache that distracts me from what I'm expected to do … Just as soon as I tried to forget you, you reappeared. No, I am not ready for that, to do that. Time will be wasted. I need to show I'm capable. The gatekeepers have an expectation I must fulfill.

Besides, I fear you will be dismissed, and I wouldn't want you to endure that pain. So, my expressive possibilities will be kept bottled. First, I must prove I'm worthy. Then, my beautiful muse, you will be able to grow wings and fly and soar over tall buildings. You will fly and have extraordinary abilities. You will fly and have exceptional skills. You will jump across the sky in a single bound and moonwalk on Mars.

3. Validation. Oh, what great news! Finally, finally, my story has been accepted. The gatekeepers have turned my pen into a wand for me to fill my journal with unseen colors, places, and sounds.

For so long I stayed frozen in a pool, in wait for the season to change and the ice that held me to thaw. Now, I get to do what I wish. This means that you get to exist.

Where did that gray cloud appear from, blocking the sun that once shone, and why do you still have that frown on your face? Never mind. I've formed a tale that will fascinate readers of any place or race. That might inspire and engage audiences long after I'm buried.

4. Where Are You? I know you are there! Why are you hiding from me again? I sat at the table with my pen and journal and waited. I called you to come, but silence answered me. Come! We have work to do— Wipe that dirt off your shoulders. I have figured out what I need you to be. You'll be the child of addicts who gains supernatural abilities. Or maybe your parents were in an involuntary experiment and you were born with superpowers. Clever ... isn't it? Why are you so unhappy? Fix your face! I need you to be happy. At least it's not a police officer beating you or a mob chasing you on an unlit street.

5. Hero. ... Finally, what took you so long? Just like you to show up when I'm at work. You usually appear when I try not to think of you. Let me look at you. Oh, that won't do ... Take it off. What happened to the jeans, red hoodie, and sneakers I gave you? ... What? No! I told you before that I can't give you a male love interest. You'll be a poor example for the children who need fathers. Our youth desperately need wholesome Black men who represent the best image of a father. ... Yes. I realize that others have been written about and have soared from print to the silver screen. But a black action hero with a dual identity and double consciousness is hard enough to squeeze into a story; I don't need to add the topic of you being queer, too.

Open your mouth and let me replace your tongue. Stop it and open it now! Do as I say! ... Wonderful. Now, say ... "Wuzz poppin'?" Right away, you sound like someone everyone will understand. Someone that all people will believe and relate to.

6. Discontent. A feeling of discontent clogs my spirit. I know what it is, but I never admit it to anyone. I'm resentful because my muse left me. At first, I spent day and night trying to find him. I scroll the files on my computer, but he is nowhere to be found. And he took the other characters that I kept hidden. It is as if they never existed. So, I wait with the hope my character—my muse, I imagine—returns to me to fill the story I've outlined.

The muses I held back are no longer pounding against my spirit to come out when I write; they have emerged in pages of books I thought would never happen. The idea I kept hidden has broken free of me to live in someone else's imagination. He's become a part of someone else's story, a part of someone else's fantasy. Did he find someone unafraid to tell his story, to let him be what he wanted?

So, now, I must go deep and pull from out my soul someone else or another story idea I've put on pause, on hold. But as much as I call, they won't come. So, I wait—just like the people I once held inside me.

7. Self Exam. A friend told me I let others wield my pen, and I must take it back. In other words, the problem wasn't me but what others expected of me. I was programmed to please a dysfunctional society. Now that I know that, I can't seem to get back to myself.

I understand my mistake now. I must embrace what is inside me, for my muse and the story I've arranged will leave and go to another land and place, to live and breathe. Other characters and places will emerge. When they come, I'll embrace them, and my muse will run, jump, then fly on my paper.

Shawn Frazier is an African American spec lit writer from Harlem where he currently lives with his dog, Yabu. He works as a High School English teacher in NYC, where he hopes one day the city will return to its glorious place it once was. Below are a few of his publications with links to his stories.

1) "The Hoodoo Nigger" was published by *Quail Bell* (http://www.quailbellmagazine.com/the-unreal/short-story-the-hoodoo-nigger).
2) His story "Jacob and The Owl" won the Mary Shelley Contest and was published in *Rosebud Magazine* issue #57 (http://www.rsbd.net/NEW/index.php?option=com_linx&Itemid=61).
3) "Nne" is featured in a special edition of *SQ Mag* (sqmag.com/2015/04/30/edition-20-nne-mother-by-shawn-frazier).
4) *Flapper House Magazine* published "How Emma Jean Crossed the River" in their #8 winter edition.
5) "Shadow's Insomnia" can be found in issue #12 of *Flapper House Magazine*.
6) "Plantation Meadows" is in the 2020 "Spec Issue" of *Middle House Review*.
7) *Drunk Monkeys Science Fiction and Fantasy* issue includes "Mountain of Joy" (https://www.drunkmonkeys.us/scifi-and-fantasy-special-issue-november-2020).
8) "In The Future Robots Will Wear a Hoodie" was published in the 2022 Fall issue of *Mizna*, guest-edited by Safia Elhillo.
9) "I See You ... and Hear You, Too," forthcoming in *The Underdog Rises*, Summer 2023.

Chinelo Onwualu is a writer, editor, and recovering journalist. She is a former co-editor of *Anathema* magazine, co-founder of *Omenana*, a magazine of African Speculative Fiction, and former chief spokesperson for the African Speculative Fiction Society. She's a 2014 graduate of the Clarion West Writers Workshop, which she attended as the recipient of the Octavia E. Butler Scholarship. Her short stories have been featured in several magazines and anthologies, including the award-winning *Africa Risen: A New Era of Speculative Fiction*, *The Saga Anthology of Science Fiction 2020*, and 2021's *Best of World SF Vol.1*. She's been nominated for the British Science Fiction Awards and the Nommo Awards for African Speculative Fiction. She's from Nigeria but lives in Toronto, Canada, and she's always happy to pet your dog.

Publishers' Note

Work on Ex Marginalia began in 2021, as Pocket Workshop was nearing its launch. Tod lived in Missoula, Huw in Seattle, and a pandemic raged. After a year of collaboration-from-afar, one chilly spring day, we met over sandwiches and wine at opposite ends of a social-distance-friendly six-foot table in Huw's backyard and sketched out the bones of this project.

As we developed a plan, it became clear that we lacked the relevant lived experiences to pursue it on our own, so first, we sought advice. Enter: Nisi Shawl, Henry Lien, and Kate Schaefer, all of whom provided not only invaluable guidance, helping to establish priorities and avoid pitfalls, but also the much-needed enthusiasm to assure us that the premise and approach were sound.

Next, we needed an editor—an inspired mind to lead the work. We made a list. It was short. At the top was someone whose work we'd followed since first meeting her as a Clarion West student in 2014; someone who'd already demonstrated passion for and expertise in everything Ex Marginalia would represent; someone equipped to summon the flesh and skin and brains and hair onto the skeleton we'd imagined—and to imbue it with life.

We asked. Chinelo said yes. And then it all happened—the recruitings, the writings, the meetings and correspondences, the edits and revisions and myriad deliberations, and the decisions—and now you hold the living, breathing, fully-formed creature in your hands.

Many others' efforts and contributions were also vital to the creation of Ex Marginalia:

Authors of Ex Marginalia—every one of you—thank you for entrusting these beautiful pieces to our care. We are honored.

Ashe Samuels, thank you for giving Ex Marginalia a face. Your cover art is brilliant, and it has been a joy to witness the evolution of this magnificent image.

Dan Trefethen and Linda Breneman, thank you for talking through financial aspects of the project with us.

Kate Dieda, thank you for proofreading. It's been a joy to work with you again. Your keen eye is matched only by your generous spirit.

Enormous thanks, Carl Brandon Society, for working to increase racial and ethnic diversity in the field of speculative fiction. Your support and collaboration made Ex Marginalia possible.

Backers and donors, you know who you are—and many of you wish to remain anonymous—but from the depths of our hearts, we thank you.

Our families—N and E for Tod; K, E, and B for Huw—thank you for your love and support ... of us and of books.

And most of all, Chinelo, thank you. Thank you for loving the idea in the first place. Thank you for your professionalism and diligence—despite illness, upheaval, and the daily demands of life. And thank you for bringing together these marvelous authors and presenting their voices to the world.

Tod McCoy and M. Huw Evans
Hydra House Books

Made in United States
Troutdale, OR
02/06/2024